D1760403

Modern Water Gardening

Modern Water Gardening

REGINALD KAYE

FABER AND FABER
3 Queen Square
London

First published in 1973
by Faber and Faber Limited
3 Queen Square London WC1
Printed in Great Britain by
Latimer Trend & Company Ltd Plymouth
All rights reserved

ISBN 0 571 08516 4

© *Reginald Kaye 1973*

Contents

"The photographs for the colour plates were taken by Mr. Harry Smith"

Illustrations

Colour Plates

Monochrome Plates

7

LINE DRAWINGS IN TEXT

Foreword

There are so many gardening books on offer that I, as an inveterate biblio-phagist, have developed a list of requirements that must be fulfilled before investing money in any work, no matter how lavishly produced.

Has the author sufficient experience of the subject to make an original contribution to the volumes already in existence? I have known Reg Kaye eighteen years and he had been gardening for thirty years before that, so all my requirements are fulfilled by that one unassailable fact.

Practical experience, no matter in what field, is dearly bought: the failures which cause the new approach to a problem, giving rise to improvization or invention, are even more important than the successes, and are what gives a book originality. There must be very few practising gardeners with the immense and varied experience of Reg Kaye in the intriguing field of water gardening, so this book will make a very real original contribution to the literature devoted already to the subject.

My own first adventure into the world of pond construction and aquatic plants is still a painful memory though thirty years have passed. I tried for three years to stop the pond leaking all over the rose garden until in fury I seized a large crowbar, broke all the concrete and made a bog garden instead. Had this book been available then I would not have made the mistakes in construction which caused my pond to leak in the first place, for Reg Kaye deals in detail with construction methods which are eminently suited to gardeners who, like myself, take pleasure in construction work. In addition there are details of what the well informed garden owner should require from a contractor hired to do the work.

Chapters on design, even on building bridges, and on pumps, heaters and circulators are all invaluable to those who are bewildered by the wealth of material available in this field.

Aquatic and waterside plants are a fascinating study, they bring a beauty, in some cases pastel shaded, in others flambuoyant, to the garden landscape. Water and the plants which enjoy growing in, or in close proximity to it, add another dimension to the garden. The book deals in detail with the planting of both outdoor and heated pools. I am stimulated into all sorts of extravagent plant purchases when reading an enthusiast's description of his favourite genera, but this is surely a sign of an author's worth that he should make his readers seize spade in hand to sally forth to make a water garden and to share with him in the delights of Nymphaea, Mentha and the whole host of plants whose very names are redolent of the romantic aura which invests every expanse of water no matter how small.

Every Eden must have a serpent. A chapter on the pests and diseases which may invade the pool to attack plants or fish is an essential not overlooked, plus practical suggestions on how the ravages they inflict can be contained or eliminated.

No man could practice gardening intelligently for fifty years and not amass a treasure house of stored information on all aspects of the art. Few men, unfortunately, have the facility to put the accumulated knowledge down on paper. Having read some of Reggie Kaye's previous literary efforts, I believe he has that ability and I wish the new venture every success.

Superintendent Harlow Car Gardens GEOFFREY SMITH
Harrogate

The Modern Water Garden

Our national hobby of gardening in Great Britain dates back to very modest beginnings in the time of the Roman occupation. The chief interest then was the provision of medicinal and culinary herbs, and these were grown in areas away from the dwelling houses of the period; even in quite recent times in Scotland the larger houses had their kail-yards where the various vegetables were cultivated. The sheets of water associated with the buildings of those days, the monastic fishponds and canals maintained for fish on Fridays, the castle moats intended to keep the neighbours away, even the village duckponds, were as purely practical as the neolithic dewponds on the South Downs.

It was only with the birth of the Renaissance in the fifteenth century that there came a great surge of interest in the more ornamental aspects of gardening, and the introduction of water became an integral part of the designs of the many immense landscaping schemes, formal and informal, brought into being as necessary adjuncts to the larger estates. Many examples still may be found in the grounds of those 'stately homes' which are still left to us, such as the lakes at Stourhead, the cascades at Chatsworth, and many others. On the Continent the architectural manipulation of water on the grand scale is a feature of many famous gardens, seen in the capitals of Europe, and the palaces of Italy, Spain and other Mediterranean countries, where the heat of the day is relieved by the play of intricate fountains, and the tinkling music of elaborate waterfalls cunningly contrived in settings of white and coloured marble, contrasted with the slender columns of Roman cypress. Today such schemes could hardly be contemplated even by the very wealthy and, indeed, however well they may have harmonized with the more elaborate architecture of their day they would not be appropriate to our modern age.

The clean lines of modern buildings demand less ornate treatment of their surroundings. Elongated rectangular panels of water set in simple frames of paving and turf, reflecting the upright lines of modern construction, with perhaps an occasional simple fountain, make a more pleasing complement to the architect's design than more elaborate treatment.

However much one may admire such settings in the larger context of public buildings, it is in the garden of the enthusiastic amateur that one finds the greatest interest in water gardening, and in particular in the aquatic plants which can be grown with its aid. Today there are hundreds—nay thousands—of keen gardeners who possess their own gardens and who would like to add some form of water garden, however small, to satisfy their ever-expanding interest in the world of plants. For almost invariably the emphasis is on the cultivation of water-lilies and other aquatic plants rather than the effect of water on the general garden scheme.

Now that the introduction of modern materials has made it possible for anyone with the available space to have a water garden without any great outlay and with very little trouble, the interest in this aspect of gardening is increasing at a fantastic rate. The advent of prefabricated pools makes it possible to decide in the morning to have a water garden, to go out and purchase one complete with a collection of suitable plants, and to install it in time to sit down and admire the addition to the garden over a cup of afternoon tea. In fact the sudden phenomenal increase in demand for water-lilies has been somewhat embarrassing to those nurserymen who specialize in growing water plants, for the propagation of water-lilies is not a rapid process, and can hardly keep pace with the demand. When concrete was almost the only material to be used in making a pool, even the smallest pool required a week to construct, followed by several weeks of seasoning before it was considered safe for the introduction of its animal and vegetable denizens. At the same time the general upheaval involved in making a concrete pool might have had its virtues by causing the owner to give a good deal of thought to the project before starting it and thereby avoiding mistakes caused by rushing the work.

SITING THE POOL

To the majority of gardeners the garden pool is so full of interest that it becomes the main centre of attraction, and if of any great extent it will dominate the rest of an average-sized garden. There are so many points to consider when it has been decided to introduce water into the garden scheme. The placing must be planned very carefully, especially if it is to be in the vicinity of buildings, for it should bear some relation to the overall design, complementary to the layout of the buildings and their surrounds. For instance, it is possible to place a pool so that it reflects some important or interesting aspect of the house or garden, so doubling the interest thereof. Or it can reflect the blue sky and, when the sun shines, throw fascinating light patterns on its surroundings. If near the house, too, its placing should be considered as a focal point of the view from the more important windows.

For the success of the plants the most important and fundamental point to observe is to site the pool where it can get the maximum sunshine possible. Six hours a day of full exposure to whatever sun there may be must be regarded as the absolute minimum when water plants are to be grown. Water-lilies especially will not flower in a shady pool, and in very shady conditions the majority of aquatic plants in general will not thrive, their growths become weakly and eventually they will die out altogether. For this reason the neighbourhood of trees, except perhaps north of the pool, should be avoided. An unseen danger from trees comes from underground, as their ever exploring and thickening roots can extend underneath and finally rupture the bottom of pools of concrete or other rigid construction—including fibre-glass.

Another trouble arising from the nearness of trees is the accumulation of fallen leaves in autumn. These rot in water, using up all the available oxygen at a time when oxygenating plants are dormant and ineffective. The rotting leaves create conditions which may be fatal to fish and detrimental to the plants, which gradually cease to thrive and may even die off during the winter. This state of affairs can be avoided if one takes the trouble to cover the pool, as soon as the leaves begin to fall, with tightly stretched netting, leaving it *in situ* until leaf-fall is complete. One-inch mesh nylon netting or one of smaller mesh is recommended. When ready the net should be gathered together from the corners, holding all the leaves, drawn away and transferred to the compost heap. This precaution is essential for the well-being of the livestock in the pool, for the scavengers in the shape of water snails, caddis larvae and the like cannot cope with a massive introduction of autumn leaves. If for any reason the use of a net has not been possible the first opportunity should be taken of raking out the accumulation of leaves, taking care not to damage the water plants. This de-oxygenation of water by rotting vegetation is the reason why the use of leafmould, peat or compost in any form should be avoided when preparing the planting medium for water plants.

Generally in the small garden there is not a great deal of latitude for siting the pool, but where there is plenty of room available, some other points will require consideration before finally deciding on the position. If the ground is quite level the question arises of how to drain away excess water. Means of emptying the pool must be thought out. If there are any land drains already existing it may be possible for the surplus to enter these, or it may be necessary to construct a soakaway as described later. Sometimes surplus water can be arranged to flow through a bog or moisture garden attached to the pool, though excess pond water usually coincides with heavy rainfall and so is not of any great advantage to the moisture garden. If an electric pump is available this can be utilized to pump away through a hose to some distant point. Baling out water is a messy business and should be avoided if the surrounds to the pool are not to be converted into a quagmire.

When the ground is sloping, provided other requirements are satisfied, the most natural place for a pool will be towards the lower part of the slope, particularly when an informal scheme is envisaged. In such a case drainage and siphoning problems are more easily solved.

Many gardeners cannot think of a pool without the introduction of a fountain of some kind. In the case of a formal garden such a feature may well prove to be interesting and attractive whether in the form of an upright play, or as a jet from some suitable figure or from a keystone in an arch. Where pools are designed to act as mirrors the play of a fountain would break up the surface and defeat the object—a placid sheet of water with interesting reflections of sky, trees and buildings. In the informal pool, however, especially one associated with a rock or woodland garden such displays are out of place, and moving water should be confined to carefully constructed streams and waterfalls. The fountain in the courtyard or patio is essentially a feature of Moorish, Spanish or Italian gardening where the coolness from evaporation is to be enjoyed in a hot and dusty climate, just as we enjoy sun-bathing in our wet one. In Britain more often we need the warmth of firesides rather than fountains, though on our occasional scorching days their sound and coolness can be welcome.

When the primary reason for having a pool is to provide an environment for cultivating water-lilies and other aquatic plants, a fountain is a mistake for, though the same water in most cases is used again and again through a pump, the effect of constant evaporation on the thousands of droplets in the jet is to lower the temperature of the water considerably. The steady growth and flowering of aquatic plants is related directly to the temperature of the water as well as to the incidence of sunlight, and the still pool therefore has the advantage in that the water temperature is built up on sunny days, with consequent improvement of growth and flowering of the plants.

The movement of water in a running stream does not result in any significant diminution of temperature, especially when the stream is being circulated through a pump. Natural streams however are, usually, far too cold for the successful cultivation of water plants excepting those native species adapted to such conditions, such as water crowfoot, potamogetons and so forth, very attractive in their proper place, but apt to take charge in the garden.

The reason why the only safe time for transplanting water-lilies and some other aquatics is early May to June is that the lengthening days and increasing hours of sunlight gradually warm up the water, stimulating and maintaining growth and root action. After midsummer day the conditions for safely transplanting water plants become more and more unfavourable as the days pass until, by the middle of August, it is extremely risky to transplant water-lilies. The longer nights and cooler days slow down growth to such a degree that the plants cannot become established before growth ceases altogether for that season. Any injured roots which have not recovered will rot away, possibly infecting the main rhizome. I have killed dozens of water plants myself by taking a chance on late transplanting—I remember buying a pool full of *Nymphaea* 'Sunrise', several dozen crowns, in late August some years ago, it being necessary to move the plants immediately. The following spring I had a collection of rotten stumps without a vestige of life in them, because I planted them in an open pool. Had I stored the crowns in damp moss in a cool, frost-proof place I might have saved them, who knows? The present value is £4 a crown!

In an artificially heated pool or in tanks under glass one might take liberties with hope of success, but not in the open-air pool. Needless to say, no aquatic plants should be disturbed during the winter months. If for any reason the pool has to be empty during the winter leave the plants *in situ* covered with bracken or similar material until the correct planting time comes along.

SOME NOTES ON DESIGN

When designing a rock and water garden with streams and falls care should be taken to place the stream so that it does not appear to spring from the highest part of the garden, a fault which is seen far too often, the idea being of course to obtain as high waterfalls as possible. This is bad design and never looks natural. It is better to place the stream so that it appears to have made its way between two rocky bluffs. It is possible, by careful planting, to suggest that the stream tumbles down from higher ground, if such there be, beyond the confines of the garden—the top of the stream should be masked by low bushes beyond which are planted shrubs which will grow progressively higher as they get farther away, finally planting two groups of trees as though the now imaginary stream flowed between them. So dominating is the appearance of water if it is more than a mere trickle that it should be regarded as the focal point of a rock garden design.

A simple stream garden can be made, of course, without any rock at all. By skilful planting an entrancing informal garden feature can be achieved where there is room to develop the idea. What could be more charming than a gently flowing stream meandering between sloping banks of ferns, with perhaps a small group of silver birches, and drifts of heaths, merging into shady portions where there are plantings of showy candelabra primulas, astilbes, spiraeas and a host of other subjects through which one may wander along paths of leafmould or peat with stepping stones across the stream here and there? Perhaps a rustic stone bridge of suitable scale could conduct the path to regions beyond the immediate view to a suggestion of woodland as background.

The formal pool often is used as the central point of a larger garden picture surrounded perhaps by formal beds of roses, or perhaps as part of a design in turf and paving with occasional formally shaped trees. So much depends on the size and type of site. The variations can be infinite, but always the pool will be the point to which one's steps naturally gravitate in search of the peace and quiet needed so much in the world today, and which one may find on contemplating the placid mirror of still water reflecting sky and trees, varied by the gentle movements of gold-fish, the lovely goblets of water-lily flowers floating serenely on the surface and the occasional sudden flash of darting dragonflies.

Though written with the purpose of encouraging the 'do it yourself' gardener to create his, or her, water garden, and thereby achieve lasting satisfaction and pride in the results, perhaps this book will be the more useful for a few observations on designing the pool. It is seldom that one finds two gardens exactly alike in spite of the uniformity of modern buildings and the restricted area usually available, and therefore each site has to be analysed carefully in order to obtain the best design for that particular site. The shape of adjacent buildings and boundaries, any existing garden layout, neighbouring trees, aspect, slope, all will have an influence which must be considered.

Generally speaking, the less complicated the design the better it will be, especially in the case of the formal pool. In the sloping garden where there is perhaps a rectangular area of paving near the house levelled to a retaining terrace wall, a simple rectangular pool, placed with its longer axis parallel to the house, as a central feature of the terrace, would be the most effective. If desired, for-mal beds for roses or for summer bedding could be arranged around the pool.

Or as a contrast to the straight lines of house and terrace wall a simple circular pool might be thought more desirable.

On a level site a long canal-like pool, which need not be more

B

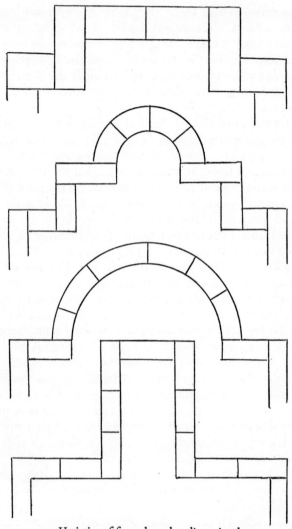

1. Varieties of formal pool endings, in plan

than 2ft. wide, with perhaps a central or terminal wider square, arranged so that the length creates a sense of distance, can be very effective.

The simpler geometrical shapes, the square, the rectangle, the circle and the elliptical or oval pool, look better and are easier to construct than more complicated ones, though a rectangular pool with semicircular ends, is a well tried and satisfying design where it fits in with the surroundings.

A useful tool to mark out a square is a right-angled triangle made from 2- × ½-in. timber so that the finished sides measure 3ft., 4ft., and 5ft., respectively; the sides can be notched at 6-in. intervals to act as a measure.

The setting out of rectangular pools is simple enough, always provided the corners are true right-angles. There is a system of designing rectangles of subtly satisfying proportions known as the square root method, which is used consistently by architects when designing rectangularly faced buildings, doorways, window spaces, towers and so forth, and by artists when composing pictures. Such rectangles are obtained by starting from a square, with a side of predetermined length, then extending one side of the square so that it measures the diagonal of the square and then completing the rectangle. The term square root rectangle comes from the fact that a square formed with a side equal to the extended base will have an area twice that of the original square. Again, if such a rectangle has its side prolonged so that it equals the length of the diagonal of the rectangle and a new rectangle set up on this side, it is known as a square root of 3 rectangle, for a square formed with the prolonged side is three times the area of the original square. This process can be extended indefinitely, the rectangles produced having very satisfying proportions.

To mark out a circle one simply hammers in a stake, preferably of circular section, at the centre point of the proposed pool, to which is attached a length of cord to act as the radius; a pointed stick is fastened to the other end. Holding the stick at right angles to the ground, walk round the stake keeping the cord taut, and scratch the circle in the ground as you go.

To mark out an oval or elliptical pool two stakes are required, set so that they are in line with the proposed length of the ellipse, and set as far apart as desired, the farther apart the more slender the resulting ellipse. The loop of cord is thrown over both stakes and on walking round with the stick and taut loop a perfect ellipse can be marked out.

Stakes about a foot apart should be driven in along the scratch to mark out the area while the mark is fresh.

The length of the loop can be adjusted to the required radius to fit the area available.

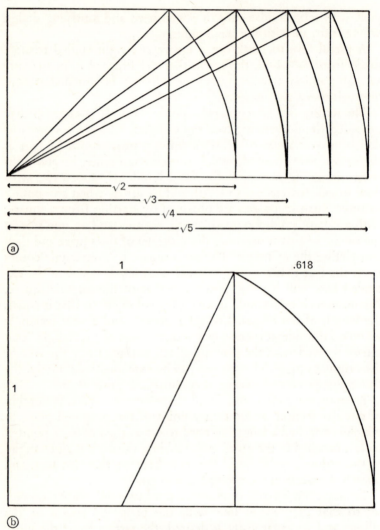

2a. Square root rectangles
2b. 'Kepler's Golden Measure' rectangle

Perhaps I should mention the 'Golden Measure' which was established empirically hundreds of years ago, but which was stated in mathematical terms by Pythagoras.

This measure is obtained from the square by bisecting one side and using the diagonal from the bisection point to the opposite angles of the square. A radius was established which when used to extend the side of the square, extended it by a length of 0·618 of the side of the square, and this length superimposed on the side of the square divided that side in the same proportion, and so on ad infinitum. The rectangle with sides 1 : 1·618 was felt to be of particularly agreeable proportions and is used constantly by artists and architects.

An effective contrast to the horizontal lines, external to the pool, can be achieved by planting one of the columnar, slower-growing conifers 2–3ft. away from one corner. The golden *Chamaecyparis lawsoniana* 'Minima Aurea' is very slow growing, and makes a fine contrast with the greys and greens of paving and pool. *Thuja plicata* 'Rogersii' is another good golden cultivar, seldom exceeding 2ft.; the ever-popular glaucous Lawson's cypress 'Ellwoodii' is no dwarf, and I have had plants which reach 10ft. in a few years' time.

Whatever the size and shape of the formal pool decided upon, one of the basic principles is to strive for a feeling of peace and repose, and this is more easily achieved by simplicity of design than by over-elaboration and the introduction of too many fussy details, architectural or horticultural.

On horizontal sites a change of levels can be had by sinking the pool a foot or so below the surrounding area, leaving room for an adequate path around the pool at water-level, and a retaining wall with steps down from the surround. If the retaining wall is finished with a coping it will provide a convenient spot for sitting to watch the fish enjoying their evolutions. Such a sunk pool is more pleasing than a raised pool. The excavated soil could be used at one end of the plot as a foundation for a rock garden, or raised beds. In all cases the pools should be excavated so as to provide varying depths of water to suit the various aquatics, 1½–2ft. for water-lilies, 3–6in. for marginal plants.

Some variations on the rectangular design are the L-shaped pool, a combination of two rectangles at right angles to one another, and the cruciform pool, usually composed of four slender rectangles meeting at a central square or circular pool, or perhaps as a simple cross. The L-shaped pool can be placed eccentrically to a system of flower beds, or to complement the angle of a building. The requirements of full exposure to sun should always be a prime consideration in placing such pools.

The informal pool is usually designed without reference to formal surroundings, buildings and so forth, it may be a simple incident amongst beds of informal planting, as a feature in an undulating lawn, or as an incident in a rock garden composition. Here the accent is on informality, and any resemblance to a symmetrical design is to be avoided. Any irregularities in the terrain should be utilized in fixing the boundaries of such a pool. Any promontories or 'capes' should have a reason, be it a small outcrop of rock, or a planting of compact dwarf shrubs or other plants, or even a grassy mound. Such promontories should have a corresponding bay on the opposite side of the pool. A still stream, i.e. an elongated stream-like pool on a horizontal site, should meander and vary in width from place to place, the inner bends being accented by waterside planting of iris and the like, the wider sections perhaps accommodating one of the smaller water-lilies. In the rock garden pool, usually the side opposite to the rocks will be kept low, with a craggy outcrop or two to accent any promontories, the rock garden side being built with bolder rock and, as recommended elsewhere, built into the pool itself.

Rock garden streams and falls should not meander to any great extent. In nature a stream through rocky country with a considerable fall, cuts its way through the softer strata more or less directly and is not turned aside except when it encounters outcrops of harder rock. Accordingly, there should be some excuse when altering the direction of a rock garden stream, such as the incidence of some strong outcrop of rock. When siting such rock garden streams it is inartistic to start the stream from the highest point of the rock garden, as is so often seen. The presence of a stream should suggest years of erosion whereby it has cut its way down amongst the rocks to its present level. For the same reason waterfalls should be recessed to some degree. These details help to give a sense of inevitability and meaning to the structure. The interest created by water is such that it must be the dominant feature of a rock garden design, and the various rock outcrops should be so placed as to balance and complement the streams framing it and the various pools without competing therewith, and so all contributing to a balanced garden picture from every aspect.

The Construction of Pools

The first matter requiring attention when making a pool is to assemble tools and materials so that they are at hand when required. In all cases the following will be needed; a good spade, a strong garden fork, a pickaxe or mattock, a sledgehammer, a wheelbarrow, planks, stout pegs, a straight-edge and a good spirit level, tape measure or measuring stick, a length of cord and a few bricks. Most of these will go into the barrow when putting under cover for the night. It can be quite frustrating when one has got to the point of starting the job to find one is held up for some tool or other, but it is always a good excuse for a tea break.

A straight-edge should be stout and rigid enough not to sag when supported at the ends only; usually timber 1in. thick, 4–5in. wide and 10–12ft. long will be adequate. To test the reliability of a straight-edge rest one end, edge up, on the ground, holding the other end up to the eye and glance along the length. Any departure from the straight will show at once. If faulty, the edge should be planed until it appears quite straight on test, making sure that any planing has not altered the even width of the timber.

Sometimes a wooden clothesprop—if such a thing exists in your establishment, and no one is looking—is straight enough for a quick check. The spirit level should be tested by placing it on a level surface so that the bubble is bisected exactly by the indicator mark on the glass tube. Reverse the level, end for end, and check that the level reads exactly the same either way about. A spirit level slightly out of kilter causes endless trouble, and the best remedy is to have it adjusted by an expert or get another one guaranteed in order.

POLYTHENE SHEETING

I suppose that the cheapest and easiest method of constructing a pool is to use polythene sheeting, particularly when a simple dish-shaped excavation is all that is desired. One simply excavates the required depression, removes any stones or hard objects which might damage the polythene film, and leaves an area at least a foot wide and quite level surrounding the cavity. This area, which forms the edges, should be beaten down to a true level, using the back of the spade for the purpose. If not truly level, the finished pool will show objectionable expanses of exposed polythene when filled. The excavated soil, if of good quality, can be used for raising mounds for a rock garden or for topping up flower beds elsewhere in the garden. Excavated soil should not be used for levelling up the edges of the pool, as it will always settle in time and upset the levels, however one beats it down.

Before placing the sheeting the surrounding edges should be checked very carefully to make sure that the pool edge is level all round. To check, establish a convenient starting point on the pool surround, by sinking a piece of board, brick or other flat object to the required level, place one end of the straight-edge, edge up, on this point and place the other end at fairly closely spaced points all around the pool perimeter with the spirit level balanced on top of the straight-edge. At each check the bubble should be bisected by the indicator mark if the ground is truly level. If incorrect, beat down the edge until true levels are established.

If the straight-edge is not long enough to reach across the pool establish a reference point in the centre of the cavity by driving in a strong stake down to the exact level, or alternatively build a pillar with bricks up to the required level, making the final adjustment with a tile, slate, or pieces of hardboard. Then the levels round the pool can be checked from the central datum point.

After checking all levels remove the stake or bricks, firm the ground and then place a smooth layer of fine builders' sand over the entire bottom, an inch thick, to protect the polythene from any sharp points which may stick up when the weight of water presses it down. Alternatively, spread a layer of dampened news-papers three or four sheets thick over the entire bottom, as smoothly as possible; the damp paper will flatten out better than if it is dry. Then the polythene sheets may be laid in position. Choose a still day for this operation, in the interests of preserving sanity. Laying polythene sheets on a windy day is a nerve-testing ordeal. The sheets should be spread as evenly as possible, neatly folding any irregularities, and the sheets should extend at least a foot over the perimeter. Each sheet should overlap its neighbour by about 1ft. Then, when the water is run in, the weight will seal the sheets together so that there is no water loss. Black is preferable to clear polythene because the latter shows up any trapped air in the form of a conspicuous silvery effect which can destroy the illusion of a natural pool.

The edge of the pool should be protected by laying suitably sized paving stones carefully fitted around the pool rim and projecting 2in over the pool edge. The stones should be wide enough to form a firm path which will not move or tip when walked upon. The joints might well be grouted with a mixture of 3 parts sand to 1 part of cement, well mixed and worked well into the joints. It should be left at least four days to harden. Alternatively, the edge of the pool might be protected with firm turf or with a combination of turf and paving stones.

If it is necessary to work within the pool the greatest care must be taken to avoid piercing the polythene with tools or boots. Only well-worn rubber boots should be worn, and care must be taken not to twist the feet about when moving around. It is better to get a strong plank long enough to reach across the pool so that it can rest on the paved edges, and reach into the pool by kneeling on or lying along the plank. In this position it is easy for the confirmed pipe smoker to drop his pipe and burn holes in the plastic film—I write from personal experience—but the hole can be sealed with a square of polythene stuck down with a suitable adhesive. When all is ready the water can be run in up to the level of the paving. Any departure from true levels will show up at once.

Such a pool should be regarded as expendable for, after two or three years, polythene begins to perish and becomes easily ruptured. Such pools have been known to last 10 years when not disturbed, but it is always better to be prepared to renew the film after two years.

VINYL SHEETING

When a more lasting job is desired some of the more sophisticated plastic products should be considered. Very satisfactory pools may be made with laminated or reinforced vinyl sheeting. In the case of these products the sheeting should be welded to the correct size by the suppliers, to whom full measurements should be sent with the order. After preparing the cavity as before, the material is stretched out horizontally over the hole, with plenty of overlap over the edge of the excavation, and well anchored around the perimeter by means of paving or other heavy stone. When it is certain that the sheet is well and truly secured water is run on to the stretched sheet. The elasticity of reinforced vinyl sheeting or plastolene is such that the weight of water causes it to sag until it follows all the contours of the cavity. As before the hole should be lined with soft builders' sand or with several sheets' thickness of dampened newspaper to make sure that no unsuspected sharp projections can pierce the sheeting. Plastolene or vinyl sheeting has a much longer life than polythene film, remaining in good condition for at least eight years, after which the material may be expected to deteriorate gradually and be liable to break up if subjected to any new strains. Undisturbed, the pool may remain satisfactory for many more years.

BUTALENE

The more recently introduced butalene or butyl rubber is a very tough material indeed. It has a laboratory-tested life of 80 years and, in fact, is used largely for lining large reservoirs where any failure of material could be very serious. This material is admirable for simply shaped pools, formal and informal; the sheets can be welded together and shaped to fit vertical-sided, rectangular pools of any size without distortion, provided that accurate measurements of the pool design are sent to the makers. The welding is a job rather outside the capabilities of the amateur, and so far there has not been offered a suitable adhesive for the home handyman.

Or this material can be used in the same way as reinforced vinyl sheeting by stretching across the pool, anchoring the edges

around the perimeter and then running in water. Actually butalene will stretch under the weight of water to fit moderately
irregular pools with no wrinkling at all whereas, usually when
plastolene is used, there may be a certain amount of wrinkling.
However, once the pool is filled, these wrinkles are of no great
importance and will not be noticed when the pool matures. A
further advantage of these reinforced vinyl and butalene sheetings
is that the informal pool may be excavated with a shallow shelf
around the sides to accommodate marginal aquatic plants, with
a deeper central area for the water-lilies, and the sheeting will
stretch to fit these contours. The sides of the excavation should
be made to slope, so that they go upwards and outwards—away
from the centre—and the junction of sides to shelf should be
rounded off.

When these products are used for rock garden pools, one side
of the pool may well be paved as outlined in the foregoing, but it
is desirable to have part of the pool edge masked with actual rock.
It is practically impossible to do this by placing rock around the
edges without showing ugly gaps below the rocks, especially
when these are laid correctly with regard to stratification. It is
better to make the shelf on the rock garden side below water
level, wide enough to accommodate these edge rocks so that they
appear to be rising from the depths. These rocks should be linked
up to rock beyond the pool edge and so mask the pool edge
completely in a natural and effective way. It would be advisable
to rest these underwater rocks on pieces of slate or cement
asbestos, wedging them firmly with small stone to eliminate
risk of damaging the sheeting.

POLAPOOL PLASTIC

Recently another highly satisfactory method of pool lining has
been developed which is efficient, inexpensive, and easy to install.
As in previous cases the excavation must be prepared with due
regard to levels, with sloping sides well beaten with the back of a
spade to make all firm and even, and any sharp projections from
stones or roots eliminated. Known as the Polapool system, all that
is required is to line the sides with hessian, the woven jute fabric
used for making sacks, backing rugs and so forth. Usually supplied in rolls 40in. wide, suitable lengths are laid down the pool

sides, allowing a foot or so beyond the pool edges. For the time being the bottom is not treated. The material is overlapped about 2in. and then in fine warm weather the fabric is coated with the special Polapool plastic, using an ordinary whitewash or similar brush. To prevent the fabric creeping under the brush, it may be temporarily secured to the firmed soil sides with large-headed, 3-in. nails, which can be removed after applying the plastic paint. Then the pool bottom is smoothed off again and well flattened, and fabric laid over the bottom, overlapping the sides by 6in., and then the bottom is treated with the same plastic paint. Finally the whole job is repainted overall and allowed to dry, after which the water can be run in.

Pools made in this way have been under test about 10 years and have given no trouble. If repairs are necessary it is a simple matter to cut a square of hessian, treat it with the plastic, cover the hole, and repaint over it. It is recommended that a refresher coat be applied to the pool every three years or thereabouts, which means cleaning out and replanting, but this chore may be advisable in any case.

There is no need to protect the pool in any way during the winter, the plastic hardens during very cold weather, and becomes pliable again with normal summer temperatures, but it is as well not to work in the pool during frosty weather just in case the hardened plastic might crack. It is recommended that in places with a high water table or with a badly drained subsoil, the base of the pool should be drained before installing the hessian. This may be achieved by taking out 6 or 9in extra depth, filling this with broken stone in which tile drains are set, topping up with stone chippings which should be well rolled in, and then blinding the top with sand on which the hessian is laid. The tile drains should be led to an existing drain or soakaway with a fall of not less than 2in. in 10ft.

This will, of course, involve digging a trench to take the tile drains before the pool is formed. The construction of a soakaway is described later on. The plastic paint is harmless to plants and fish when dried—each coat will take about three days to dry in fine weather.

FIBRE-GLASS POOLS

Prefabricated fibre-glass pools are very popular nowadays and are made in many designs by several specialist firms. Formal and informal shapes are offered; even prefabricated rock waterfalls and streams are being made in fibre-glass, and they are by no means a bad imitation of the real thing, though not easy to mask really convincingly. The greatest fault with the present standard fibre-glass pools is that they are not deep enough for use in any serious water-gardening scheme, but they are excellent for modest layouts in the modern small garden where their limitations are acceptable.

Installation is simple. Again it is as well to bed the fibre-glass pool in soft sand, gently ramming all round it, but taking care to maintain a dead level. A pool cocked up at one end destroys at once any sense of a natural appearance, and is a perennial eyesore. When firming the soil go round and round, gradually filling up and checking constantly to see that, inadvertently, the ramming has not pushed one or other side up above level. After a few years a fibre-glass pool will become brittle and will require care when doing any maintenance work. Ten years is an average life, though with care they will last twice as long. They are a good deal more expensive than the plastic and butalene liners, size for size.

PUDDLED CLAY POOLS

The puddled clay pool is not given much attention these days, but in a district where clay abounds and where expense is a consideration, it is by no means to be despised. The first water-lily pool I ever made was in the Colne valley, where below a superficial 6in. of good, dark, garden soil, there lay indefinite depths of a particularly dense yellow clay with occasional bluish variegations. One simply skimmed off the topsoil beyond the limits of the pool to be dug, and down to the required depth, using the excavated blocks of clay to build up the sides to the required level, beating them with a wooden mallet to a thickness of a foot or so. When the required depth was achieved, the surface was smoothed off by repeated beatings and working with the back of a spade until a perfectly smooth homogeneous surface was made.

Paving around the edges with the local stone flags made a good firm path. On filling such a pool, at first the water will be full of minute clay particles and look rather like a bath of mustard. These particles never settle without assistance. This is effected by slaking one or two cobs of burnt lime in a plastic bucket (galvanized buckets are attacked by fresh lime), and the clear liquid, containing calcium hydroxide, is distributed over the pool surface through a plastic rosed watering-can. The result is that the lime flocculates the fine particles into larger aggregates which settle quickly, leaving perfectly clear water. Quite recently I saw this pool in perfect condition 30 years after I had made it.

A formal pool of puddled clay should have the sides lined with brick or stone walling to maintain a sharp clean line. How well I recall that clay subsoil where I started my gardening career over 50 years ago. When one had cut a particularly fine lump of clay and attempted to throw it to one side, as often as not it refused to leave the spade, and one was pulled after it willy-nilly. Yet some very good plants were grown in the dark topsoil overlaying that too, too, solid clay, better plants than I can grow now on my well-drained, light loam over limestone.

CONTAINER POOLS

Where space is very limited, some charming little pools can be made by utilizing tubs or half casks. These should be sunk into the ground to within an inch of the rim. If sunk down to the rim, muddy surface soil may wash in with the rain. Such a tub would accommodate one of the smaller water-lilies and two or three not too-strong-growing marginals. The edges could be masked with paving stones, or rocks, and suitable plants such as mimulus in its many coloured varieties, all manner of creeping rock plants, even a gunnera if one uses the creeping *Gunnera magellanica*, a dwarf relative of the giant gunnera which is such a feature of some of the larger water gardens in our public parks and botanic gardens. The dwarf gunnera is quite hardy, requiring no winter protection as is the case with its giant cousins.

There is no reason why two or three or several such tubs should not be worked into a very pleasing form of water garden, whether with a formal layout of paving, or as incidents in an informal scheme, interspersed with dwarf conifers and dwarf flowering shrubs of compact habit, not growing so large as to shade the water. Primulas, astilbes, spiraeas and many other moisture-loving plants would give added colour before the water-lilies begin their display. A different set of plants could be grown in each tub, carefully selecting those dwarf water-lilies which would be happy in such confined quarters. Care should be given to the selection of other aquatics so that they do not grow too large, preventing a sight of the water and any fish therein.

Incidentally, the inclusion of fish, apart from their interest and beauty, is a guarantee against the subsequent development of midge and mosquito larvae, for such containers are ideal breeding grounds for these pests which are ideal fish food.

Tubs made from discarded wine casks or beer barrels are ideal; any which may have contained petrol, oil, tar or allied substances should not be used unless they have been well cleaned out and charred with a blowlamp until all traces of the former contents have been eliminated, for such materials are poison to animal and vegetable life alike. After charring, fill the tubs with water and allow to stand for a few days. If an iridescent film appears on the water surface this indicates that there is still dangerous contamination seeping out from the barrel staves, and the tubs will not be safe for planting. After drying, a further charring should remove the contamination, but if, after testing, traces of surface film still appear, it is safer to discard such barrels so far as water gardening is concerned. Tubs which have dried out frequently leak when first filled, but usually the staves swell up after a time and the tub becomes watertight. If not, a little clay worked into a putty-like consistency and rubbed into the joints generally seal the leaks permanently if the vessel is not allowed to dry out again.

When installing tubs in the garden, holes slightly deeper than the tubs should be dug out, and soft soil free of stones should then be scattered in the bottom of the hole and trodden firm to such a level that, when the tub is in position, its rim is 1in. above ground level. Then more soil should be packed firmly round the tub, tamping down with a pick handle or similar tool, so that the tub is held quite firmly to resist pressure from within when the water is frozen. Check frequently with the spirit level in case the firming process tilts the tub.

In fact, any clean container which will hold water and which is deep enough for the well-being of aquatic plants can be brought into service. Old stone troughs, if deep enough and of good size, make most attractive water gardens, even old baths need not be despised if they can be well camouflaged. It is even possible to grow one or two of the pygmy water-lilies within the house itself in a sunny window if a watertight container, 6–9in. deep is available—the deeper size being preferable. All that is needed is 3–4in. of good loamy soil mixed with a little granulated charcoal in the bottom and the container filled with water. The water-lily crown is planted in the loam with the growing point just showing. Such a plant should produce several flowers about an inch in diameter during the summer months. Even a deep bulb bowl would answer the purpose. During the winter months the bowl and contents should be kept wet in a cold but frost-free place; the following spring the container should be washed out and the lily planted in fresh soil ready for another summer's blooming.

Even if the reader is a flat dweller or has no garden where he can give rein to his urge to grow a few aquatic plants, there is no reason why he should not enjoy a miniature water garden. It should be possible to fit up a window box on a sunny windowsill with a plastic or other waterproof lining and, provided that at least 6in. internal depth is available, 3in. of which should be filled with good loam and the rest of the container then filled with water, quite a nice selection of the more dwarf water plants could be grown: a pygmy lily, dwarf acorus, *Typha minima*, frogbit (*Hydrocharis morsus-ranae*) and, of course, one or two small fish to maintain a balanced system and deal with the midge problem.

LEVELLING

I have mentioned several times the importance of checking levels constantly when making a pool. Especially with an extensive pool, it is quite easy to be a fraction of an inch out, with a straight-edge, and this error can be multiplied and add up to inches when

---

I. Barnsley House. Nicely contrasted vertical and horizontal planting design, but the Nymphaeas are badly overgrown

II. The Giant Gunnera in early summer contrasts superbly with other waterside subjects at Brodick Gardens, Scotland

the straight-edge is moved from point to point round a large excavation. A useful check can be made by using a transparent plastic hose, or any hose with glass or other transparent tubes inserted firmly in the ends. The hose should be filled completely with water, and one end fixed to an upright stake inside the excavation, so that the water level corresponds with that of the finished pool. The other end kept upright can be moved to any part of the pool, and the water in the hose will come up to the required level, provided that the hose is full of water with no air locks.

LARGE POOLS

For the larger pool or artificial lake where it is required to grow many kinds of water-lily, landscaping the margins with drifts of moisture-loving subjects, the choice of materials falls between the more permanent butalene, or concrete. There is no doubt that butalene is an ideal material for making quickly an extensive and straightforward water garden, for it can be welded together by the makers to form an impervious layer of any size, one which has the elasticity to adapt itself to all the varied contours of the excavation and once in position will last a lifetime. Once one has determined on the shape of the pool, this should be marked out with pegs joined with a stout line. A useful tool for establishing flowing curves is a long hosepipe, this lends itself to form evenly curving lines without kinking or other trouble.

When fixing the area for a large pool the building up of the edges above the undisturbed ground is to be deprecated unless of very minor extent, for disturbed ground always settles after some weeks of weathering, even when originally rammed hard on placing. Far better to make use of the natural contours of the ground to obtain an interesting shape which will look as though it had happened naturally. When excavating such a pool, the depth should be varied, leaving shelves around the margins some 9in. below the planned water surface to provide planting areas for marginal aquatics. These shelves should be varied in width from $1\frac{1}{2}$ to 3–4ft., according to the area of the pool. The deeper parts of the pool should vary from $1\frac{1}{2}$–4ft., the greater depth being recommended when the stronger water-lilies are to be grown—such a cultivar as *Nymphaea tuberosa* 'Poestlingberg' is better grown in even deeper water, when more and larger flowers will

c

be produced. By the way, if the pool is to be made of concrete an extra 6in. depth must be allowed to take the thickness of concrete.

It is stated in some quarters that 1½ft. is quite deep enough for growing water plants and this is correct, especially in water plant nurseries where the important thing is to be able to get plant orders out quickly. The plants grow faster in the shallow water, as it warms up more quickly than deeper water, but the strong-growing water-lilies should have deeper water for their permanent quarters, for their leaves spread out too far in shallower conditions. Furthermore, those water-lilies which are adapted to deeper water produce better and larger flowers when planted at their correct depth. When these strong-growing varieties are well established in a shallow pool their foliage grows right out of the water so thickly that the leaves cannot float on the surface, a mass of foliage and few flowers are produced, and it becomes necessary to lift and divide the plants much more often than if the plants were placed at their correct depth in the first place. The finest stand of *Nymphaea × marliacea* 'Chromatella' I ever saw was lining the margin of the lake at Spetchley Park in water 4–5ft. deep, a colony of about a hundred yards in length and perhaps 10ft. wide, and there were at least seven to eight flowers out continuously for every square yard of the surface.

Another reason for providing sufficient depth for the stronger water-lilies is to allow room for an adequate bulk of growing medium. The plastic planting crates so popular at the present time hold enough soil for the more dwarf varieties to thrive for a season or two, or for starting the stronger lilies when they are to be lowered on to a greater body of soil on the pond bottom. As a permanent home for the stronger lilies, they are useless, for these require something like 10cu. ft. of soil each to keep them in robust health for any length of time. Insufficient soil results in dwarfed growth and a meagre display of flowers. Planting areas 1yd. square and 1ft. deep should be provided on the pond bottom for these strong growers. The soil may be contained by three courses of brick laid without mortar or by a bottomless box of strong boards. Alternatively the whole pool bottom may be covered with strong turfy loam (i.e. that derived from rotted down turf, or the topsoil just below the turf of meadowland) to a depth of at least 9in. When one needs to move about the pool amongst the plants the built containers are better, for then one does not stir up so much mud. It is rather embarrassing wading through 9in. of wet soil when one's boots are drawn off by the suction, and one overbalances and communes with the fish.

Concrete Pools and Streams

When a fairly ambitious scheme is envisaged, for instance, of a large rock garden with stream, waterfalls and pools, modern plastic materials are not so suitable, and concrete is the more flexible medium for, apart from the difficulty in arranging plastic sheeting to follow winding streams, to construct such streams and waterfalls with rocks placed naturally so as to present a convincing picture, a really substantial foundation on which rocks can be moved about is required.

After some 40 years and more experience in making rock and water gardens, I have evolved the following method which I have found to be the most satisfactory. Before any rock is placed, the outline of the stream is marked out and made twice as wide as the finished stream is to appear. The foundation for the concrete must be placed on undisturbed subsoil, or built up to the required height with brick or stone walling, filled in between with hard core, broken brick or other hard material well consolidated as it is introduced. Concrete laid on made-up soil without such preparation is bound to break up sooner or later because made-up soil settles slowly for months, however hard it is rammed. I well remember being asked to give evidence as an expert witness in a case where a firm had built such a concrete stream on a made-up mound which had been bulldozed to one end of the garden. When I saw the results, it was possible to see daylight under the concrete where the soil had settled, leaving the concrete in mid-air. Of course it had fractured in several places, and the whole job had to be done again properly.

Having built up the foundation solid to the concrete level, the water channel is made with strong sides not less than 6in. above the stream bed and at least 3in. above the planned water level

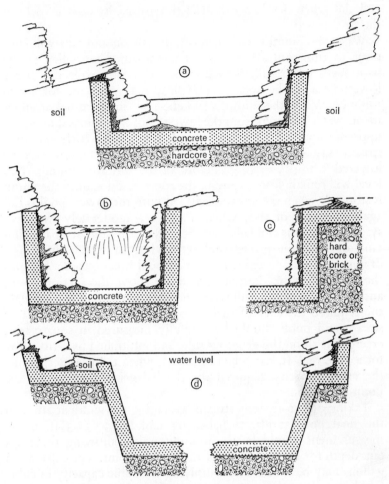

3a. Section of concrete stream bed showing method of masking by means
of suitable rocks cemented in place
3b. c. Sections showing method of masking concrete waterfall
3d. Method of masking concrete pool (section)

when the stream is running. The height of the water level when
running, above that when the stream is stopped, depends on the
volume supplied by the pump used, and also on the width of the
stream at any given point, but on average one should allow for at
least 2in. rise when the water is running in unrestricted sections,

and 3in. when the flow is restricted by obstacles such as rocks in the stream bed.

When the pump is switched off, the stream and falls will continue to run until all sections of the stream have fallen to the basic level when still, the excess water having collected in the lowest pool in the system. This flow may continue for 15–20 minutes. When the pump is switched on, in the usual arrangement, water is drawn from the lowest pool and pumped up to the uppermost part of the watercourse. In the case of a fairly extensive stream, say 50ft. or so, the level in the lowest pool may be lowered 3 or 4in. or more before all the falls are running. This level will remain low, exposing the concrete sides, until the pump is stopped, when the streams will fall until the lowest pool is full again. Because of this, where there is a moderately extensive system of streams and falls, I advocate the provision of a balancing tank or reservoir placed underground from which the pump draws the water. In effect the lowest pool functions as a fall into the balancing tank, keeping the water above the suction point, and always remaining full when the water is running. To estimate the required capacity of such a balancing tank the total area of stream and pools should be carefully measured in square feet, erring if at all on the generous side, and multiplied by $\frac{1}{4}$ (to allow for a 3-in. or $\frac{1}{4}$-ft. rise when running), when the product will be the cubic capacity required for the balancing tank above the point of suction.

Taking our 50-ft.-long stream, averaging the width at 2ft., and the final pool at 8ft., a balancing tank of $3 \times 3 \times 3\frac{1}{2}$ ft. inside measurement would be the minimum size, allowing the extra 6in. depth for the water below the suction point. The capacity in gallons may be found by multiplying the cubic capacity in cubic feet by $6\frac{1}{4}$. It may be assumed, therefore, that some 200 gallons of water will be required to lift all the streams and pool from still to running level. When the pump is switched off, the excess water drains into the balancing tank, filling it to the top. To be on the safe side, it is as well to make the balancing tank 25 per cent larger than the estimated size, and it should be kept quite full when the pump is not working. Also, before switching on, make sure that any water losses through evaporation or other cause have been made good throughout the system, for it is very detrimental for the pump to run dry.

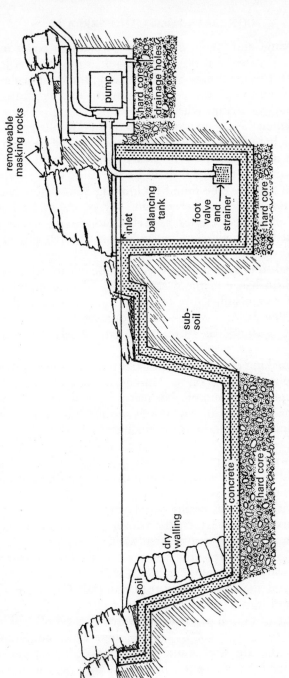

4. Section of concrete pool with balancing tank and pump house showing masking with suitable stone

The streams and pool are filled up by running water into the top of the system until the lowest pool begins to overflow. If, after the stream is running at full capacity, the level in the reservoir continues to fall, this certainly points to an overflow somewhere along the stream when it is running, though there may be no losses when the stream is still. Or it is just possible that there is a leak in the hose from the pump to the stream top, though this is unlikely if installed correctly. Usually failure to build up the concrete stream sides sufficiently will be the cause of the water loss, and such a leak may be found by looking for a place where the soil adjoining the stream is becoming excessively moist. In such a case the concrete edge must be well cleaned with a wire brush, and notched with a chisel to key additional concrete placed above the low section.

If the leak is in such a place that it is difficult to get at without a major disturbance to the rock building, it may be possible to lower the stream sufficiently by using thinner stone at the lip of the fall. The latter may be the more satisfactory method if the rock masking the stream is completely masking the concrete.

When making concrete streams and pools it is penny-wise and pound foolish to skimp on the amount of concrete used. A good deal depends on the subsoil. For instance in the case of one pool I made, the whole affair was cut out of solid limestone, and there was no point in using a great thickness of concrete, a trowel rendering of fine waterproof concrete 1in. thick was quite adequate. On the other hand, on loose gravelly soils a thickness of 6in. should be regarded as a minimum and reinforcing material should be used, for stresses are likely to be great during very frosty weather. Water drains rapidly through gravel, and when frost comes in dry weather, the frozen gravelly soil is likely to have a lower pressure than the ice within the pool.

Again, in a heavy retentive soil the pressures of the frozen surrounding soil and that of the pond ice are likely to be more or less balanced and the risk of fracture is reduced. One cannot compromise with the tremendous pressure exerted by frozen ground and because of this, in part, I evolved my method of masking the edges of streams and pools by making these wide enough to build up rock within the stream and pool edges so that the entire base of each stone is set in concrete integrated with the concrete of the stream bed and pool shelf. Any attempt to mask the edges with rock, partly set on the concrete edge and partly resting on the adjacent soil, is to court failure because the first severe frost will exert a great lifting pressure, effectively breaking away any such pieces of rock from the concrete edge and perhaps damaging the latter below water level. To be effective, masking stones must have their bases below the water level. Nothing is more destructive of a natural effect than a severely horizontal rim showing beneath a row of indifferently set stones balanced thereon. In the case of a formal concrete pool with a paved edge I recommend for the same reason that the whole row of paving stones adjacent to the pool be set in concrete integrated with the pool concrete for their entire width.

It is possible and desirable to diversify the edge of a rock pool by an occasional drift of pebbles or gravel sloping into the pool, provided that it covers the edges deeply enough. Turf can be used to mask the edges when the ground is level, but it is not recommended to lay turf down a slope into a pool, as, apart from the difficulty in keeping the grass trim, it becomes waterlogged and affords dangerously slippery footing. When making informal concrete pools, the sides should be sloping, so that they go upwards and outwards from the pool centre at an angle of 45 degrees. This enables the concrete to be placed in position without the need for formers or shuttering, and also reduces the pressure exerted by ice on the pool-sides in hard weather—not that the ice will slip up the slope as is sometimes stated, but pressure at right angles is avoided. The sloping sides also reduce the volume of water and therefore the latter warms up a little more quickly in summer.

When a formal pool is to be made, usually vertical sides are specified, though this is not essential. When the surrounding soil is of stiff heavy consistency it is quite practicable to dig out satisfactory excavations for lining with one of the plastic liners without any further work, but where the soil is loose or gravel, it is almost impossible to maintain a vertical side without some form of solid support. In the latter case, when it is desired to use some form of plastic liner it is advisable to construct the sides sloping at the angle of rest, or less, and the formal outline achieved by using paving cut to an edge, straight or curved, according to the particular design. When a vertically-sided design is demanded for small installations, the formal fibre-glass pool no doubt is adequate, but in the case of more ambitious schemes some means must be devised for maintaining the vertical sides. Practically speaking, the choice lies between brickwork, masonry or concrete. Unless second-hand building stone can be obtained from the demolition of old buildings, the cost of masonry may be prohibitive, though properly built stone walls of adequate strength made with cement mortar will be excellent. It is necessary only for the exposed inner walls to be made of dressed stone; the external walls adjacent to the surrounding soil may be built with rougher stone, but all interstices must be filled with cement mortar, being careful to leave no cavities. The double-sided wall is recommended for the larger formal pools, but moderate-sized pools can be quite satisfactory, made with a single stone face backed with concrete carefully worked until it is quite solid, as the walling proceeds, all the crevices and joints being carefully made with cement mortar, leaving no gaps.

Brick walls always should be built double, English bond being regarded as the strongest method. Very great care must be taken to ensure that there are no gaps in the jointing, and the faces should be cement rendered afterwards to make sure that they are watertight. There is no virtue in having the brick face showing below the water for aesthetic reasons—it will become covered with minute vegetation as the pond matures and this masks completely the kind of material used. Apart from scrubbing-off being a never-ending and unnecessary task, this vegetation is part of the maturing process and is a valuable factor in maintaining a healthy pool balanced for plants and animal life. Of course, artificial pools intended for swimming must be kept clean and all vegetation should be excluded from them, but such pools are in a different category, beyond the scope of this book. We are dealing with ornamental pools whose main purpose is for the growing of aquatic plants and the more natural conditions we can achieve, the better.

Both stone and brick walls should be finished off and sealed from the elements by means of a stone coping, of flat flags or moulded stone according to the requirements of the design. Perhaps it should be mentioned that the bricks chosen must be those made for outdoor use; some types of brick, while quite satisfactory for interior work, will gradually disintegrate under the influence of frost. Concrete bricks are perfectly safe. Concrete blocks, each the equivalent of six common bricks, can be built more quickly, and these also should be built double and cement rendered. They should be made from gravel, sand and cement— the so-called breeze blocks made from coke debris, intended for interior use, should not be used. These precast concrete blocks can be obtained with 'tongue and groove' ends to key them together, and this type is preferable to the plain type for this kind of work.

There remains the construction with concrete, and when vertical pool sides are required a mould must be made with 'shuttering'. Again, when the cavity is dug out of heavy stiff ground, shuttering for the inside of the pool is all that is required, the cavity being made wide enough to allow of 6in of concrete all. round. The concrete bottom is laid and allowed to harden for two or three days, then the shuttering is placed in position and the concrete placed—placed, not thrown—for throwing the concrete causes the aggregate to separate from the finer material and weakens the work. When the pool is to be dug out of loose or gravelly soil, double shuttering will be required, and the soil must be dug out far enough back from the hole to obviate any chance of loose soil or gravel running down the sides into the place where the concrete walls are to be set.

As before, first the bottom should be laid, and in the case of gravelly subsoil or in fact any subsoil that is not very hard, a layer of hard core or broken stone 3 or 4in. thick should be well rammed into it to a level finish and the concrete placed on top of this, introducing at the same time any reinforcing material. In the case of a clay subsoil which may crack in dry weather, a similar layer of hard core should be used, as it insulates the concrete from the cracking clay.

Shuttering consists of panels made up from 1-in. boards fastened together by nailing battens across the width of the panel, every 3 or 4ft. like the top of a trestle table—and made as wide as the pool is to be deep, and as long as needed. In the case of large pools more than one panel may be needed for each side, for ease of handling. The panels for the pool ends should be made just long enough to fit *inside* those for the pool sides. Where double shuttering is required the same procedure is followed, making the panels for the outer sides longer to allow for the thickness of con-

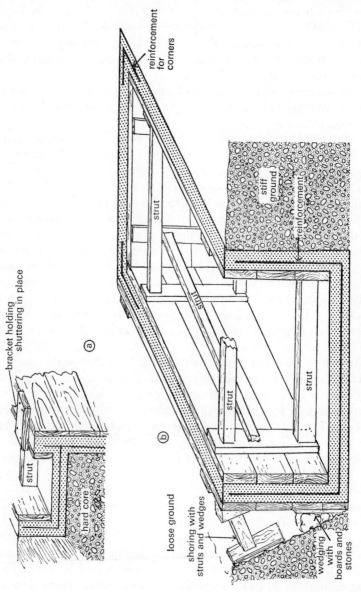

bracket holding
shuttering in place

strut

(a)

hard core

(b)

reinforcement
for corners

strut

struts

stiff
ground

reinforcement

strut

strut

loose ground

shoring with
struts and wedges

wedging with
boards and
stones

5. Details of shuttering for formal concrete pool

crete and, of course, for the thickness of the end panels which are to fit inside the side panels.

The shuttering is set up and held in place, in the case of the outer panels, by driving 3 × 3-in. thick stakes outside the panels, every 3 or 4ft., taking care to get them perpendicular, in contact with the panels. Incidentally, it is not necessary to use good 1-in. boards for the outer panels; panels made up from old packing cases, second-hand asbestos cement sheets, corrugated iron and so on can be used and regarded as expendable, leaving them in position after the concrete has set. The stakes, however, should be removed three or four days after the concrete has been placed.

The inner panels are set up, with the smooth sides in contact with the concrete; they are held in position at the bottom by stout timbers wedging the opposite sides apart at the right distance, and at the top by battens nailed into the top boards of the panels, leaving the nails not quite driven home so that they can be extracted easily after the concrete has set. These battens, of course, should reach across the pool in one piece. The joins of the side and end panels are held secure and square by diagonal battens nailed across the corners. At all stages constant tests should be made to check verticals and levels. To prevent concrete sticking to the panels they should be painted with old sump oil or well rubbed with soap, before erecting.

It is wise to reinforce concrete work for garden pools and this may be done by using standard reinforcing steel mesh, or pencil-thick steel rods laid in a lattice pattern on the bottom, wired together where they cross one another, and turned up at right angles where they enter the sides. Or heavy-gauge pig netting may be used. Wire netting is not so good and must be wide mesh, heavy gauge, if used, so that the concrete can bond together perfectly through the mesh. The reinforcement is put in position after a 2-in. thickness of concrete has been laid, the additional 4-in. thickness being placed immediately the reinforcement is in position. The concrete must be well tamped down to ensure perfect bonding through the meshes. The ends of reinforcement rods which have been turned up to key into the sides should be sited half way through the thickness of the sides, and additional steel rods should be fixed diagonally in a diamond mesh, to reinforce the sides. The corners should have right-angled rods set into the concrete every 6in. or so to help bind the corners together.

Three or four days after the concrete has set, the shuttering should be removed by withdrawing the nails holding the fixing battens from the top of the sides and corners, and removing the battens. Then the timbers wedging the bottom should be worked out, and finally the panels worked loose, the end panels first and then the side panels.

The surface of the concrete should then be well rubbed down with a flat stone or with an old leather rasp to remove any excrescences, brushed off, and then rendered with strong cement rendering made with 3 parts fine sand to 1 part of cement. This rendering is smoothed on about ½in. thick with a 'float', and finally smoothed when half set with a damp brush or cloth. This seals any minute holes left in the concrete surface.

MIXING AND PLACING CONCRETE

Sufficient concrete should be mixed to lay the pool floor in one operation, and after three or four days the shuttering for the sides is put into position and carefully checked to ensure that all is correctly placed before the concrete for the sides is mixed. The concrete for the sides also should be placed in one operation; concrete begins to set within half an hour of mixing and it is important that it is placed as quickly as possible after mixing, so enough must be mixed to complete the sides all at once. Joining freshly mixed concrete to concrete which has already set lays the foundation for future trouble, for such joints are always weaker than one completed at one time. As the concrete is placed between the shuttering it should be tamped down gently to ensure that all cavities are eliminated.

When the time comes for concreting, it is as well to assemble a band of willing helpers so that all can proceed quickly. Concrete can be purchased ready mixed and delivered on site ready to place. Sometimes it is possible to get the vehicle right up to the work, and the freshly mixed concrete is delivered by a shute, directly between the shuttering so that the job can be finished in a matter of minutes. More often, the mix must be deposited on a suitably hard, smooth surface and brought to the pool in barrows, and here the helpers prove their worth—or otherwise—a team of five with two barrows makes light work, two men to a barrow, the odd man, preferably the owner of the pool, tamping down the concrete as it is placed and controlling the pace. The usual load for a mixer is in the neighbourhood of 4 tons, and such a team should manage to clear such a load in under an hour.

The standard concrete mix is 3 parts clean gravel, 2 parts sharp sand and 1 part cement, mixed with enough water to render the mix plastic and workable without being sloppy. Only the best fresh cement should be used. Cement which has been stored some time is apt to deteriorate and become lumpy, and is then useless for pond making. The concrete can be mixed with a water-proofing compound and the latter should be incorporated in the final rendering. The suppliers of ready-mixed cement will add waterproofing, or anti-freeze or rapid-setting materials at re-quest, but it is most important to get such mixtures placed with a minimum of delay or you may find the concrete setting in the barrows before the load is dealt with. One of the hardening and sealing compounds should be brushed over the rendering before it gets quite hard; this creates a flint-hard surface and also seals in some of the harmful chemicals. As an old helper of mine used to say: 'It takes the fire out of it.'

By the way, the reason that fine sand is specified for rendering is that any tiny pebbles invariably trip up the float and create holes in the surface most aggravating to eliminate.

If the concrete is to be mixed by hand it is as well to mix the required amount dry, on a suitably hard surface, such as a garage floor—taking care that any drains are covered so that they do not get blocked—and have your assistants make the concrete with just enough water applied through the rose of a watering-can to render the mix workable, in such amounts that a steady supply to the pool can be maintained. Applying water through a hose separates the aggregate from the finer portions and involves much spadework to create a homogeneous mixture.

To summarize, the mix is 3 parts clean gravel (aggregate) $\frac{1}{2}$–1in. grade, 2 parts sharp sand, 1 part fresh cement, all by volume. To arrive at the required quantity of concrete multiply the height, length and breadth (thickness) of the walls, sides and bottom, in feet and divide the figures obtained by 27. This gives the cubic yards required. For instance, a pool 3ft. deep, 18ft. long and 9ft. wide with 6in. walls would require 3cu. yd. of concrete for the walls, and a further 3cu. yd. for the floor.

2 ($18 \times 3 \times \frac{1}{2}$ft.) (twice for two sides)   ..   54cu. ft.
2 ($9 \times 3 \times \frac{1}{2}$ft.) (twice for the ends) ..   ..   27cu. ft.
$18 \times 9 \times \frac{1}{2}$ft. (once for the bottom) ..   ..   81cu. ft.

Divided by 27 this gives 3cu. yd. for the sides and a further 3cu. yd. for the bottom—ready-mixed cement suppliers work in cubic yards.

In cool weather the concrete can be left to harden naturally, but in hot, dry weather the hardening should be delayed by covering the work with damp sacking and keeping it damp for four or five days. As soon as the concrete is hard enough to withstand gentle rubbing with a piece of wood the pool should be filled and left for a few days, for excess lime to diffuse out into the water—very alkaline water is deadly to animal and vegetable aquatics. If a hardening agent has been applied to the final coat of concrete the one soaking may be sufficient. The pool is then emptied and washed down with a soft brush and refilled. After two or three days the water can be tested for alkalinity with litmus paper or with a pH testing kit. If the water is not alkaline the pool will be safe for planting—remembering that aquatics should not be planted before April or after mid-July.

If the pool has been constructed during the autumn or winter months, after the first soaking it should be emptied and left for the rain to wash out any remaining alkali, and will then be ready for planting in the spring after a clean out and refilling. In the case of a spring-constructed pool, the neutralization of the alkali may be effected by various methods. One is to dissolve enough potassium permanganate to make the water a deep purple, leave it for a few days, empty, wash down and refill. I know of no reason why this should be satisfactory but it seems to be so. I have used it several times with complete success. Another method is to add acetic acid to the second filling until the water shows a *slight* acid reaction. It should again be emptied, washed down, and refilled and tested. Acetic acid is the active principle in vinegar, but the latter is only a very weak solution. The use of other acids is not recommended, as they are far too dangerous in unskilled hands and they may leave harmful residues, or attack the concrete itself.

The pool just described is a simple rectangular affair of uniform depth. It is probable that the designer will require planting areas for marginal aquatics and it is very little extra trouble to adapt the shuttering to provide such areas, remembering that the base on which the concrete is to be laid must be of hard core for the shallow parts as well as for the bottom. Or it may be desired to have a pool with semicircular ends or a combination of curved and straight ends. I have found the best method of making formers for such curved work is to bend hardboard to the desired curve, nailing it to adjacent panels and holding it to the required curve with timber shores. Or thin, oiled, 3-ply wood may serve. After the concrete has set the hardboard can be prised away from the panels with little trouble.

THE RAISED POOL

Where informal schemes are being constructed the raised pool is not in keeping with such designs and will look wrong, but for a formal layout there is no reason why pools should not be made with raised copings or dwarf walls above ground level. Obviously it is impracticable to build raised edges to plastic-lined pools, for the weight of dwarf walls demands a firm and solid foundation. Therefore, raised pools must be built with concrete, brick or masonry, and the thickness of the walls should be at least 9in. well reinforced. The maximum height of such walls above ground level will depend of course on the wishes of the designer, but I recommend that sitting height should be regarded as a maximum above ground level. If the level of the water is to be above ground level the walls will not have the balancing pressure of the ground to withstand strains inevitable from ice, and therefore faultless construction is essential. In areas where keen frosts are the rule a 9-in. wall might not be sufficiently strong and 12, or 18in. in the case of masonry walls, should be specified. The longer the walls of the pool the more important it is to build really strongly. All walls should be capped with copings to prevent water getting into the joints of the building, as well as providing a good finish.

BUILDING BRIDGES IN THE WATER GARDEN

In the days of my youth I remember reading *De Bello Gallico*, in which a man called Caesar made a habit of throwing bridges over rivers. Not for ornament, however. When a stream in the garden

D

is rather long and more than 2ft. wide, usually some means of crossing dryshod is desirable, as well as increasing interest. The simplest method would be to set one or two stepping-stones in the bed of the stream. When the stream has been constructed with concrete it is a simple matter to cement stepping-stones in firmly. If the stream is formed with plastic lining it is almost impossible to provide firm stepping-stones, and unless one rejoices in the spectacle of some visitor unsuccessfully endeavouring to retain his balance before he falls in the water, it is better to bridge the stream. The simplest bridges consist solely of slabs of stone long enough to span the stream, and bed down firmly in the ground on either side. If natural-surfaced stone is used, it will fit in well with informal planting. If the stream is fairly wide it might be necessary to use two or more slabs, the joints resting on pillars of stone or on single large stones set in the stream after the style of the old 'clapper' bridges.

In moderate-sized gardens such bridges are better than more pretentious structures, but in the case of a really extensive water garden where more important paths have to cross the stream, more substantial bridges will be required. Probably the easiest and simplest method is to set two or more strong wooden beams across the stream, checking that they are level. Strong boards are then firmly nailed edge to edge across the beams, at right angles to the path. A carefully secured handrail will be of assistance to elderly persons using the bridge. Timber bridges have a limited life before they require repair or renewal. For those who like to exercise their skill with stone it is great fun making an arched stone bridge. In the informal garden, natural-faced walling stone gives the best appearance, and usually the local stone will serve if it is sufficiently durable.

If the stream is already in existence when it is decided to build such a bridge, a wooden former will be required, built to fit the arch required. Two formers, one for either side of the bridge will be necessary. Made from 1½-in. planks nailed to battens and sawn to the correct curve, they are set up as far apart as the required width of the bridge, allowing for the building of walls over the bridge, and joined by boards at right angles, the width of the bridge, nailed edge to edge the full length of the arch. The boards must be strong enough to take the weight of the stone to be used without sagging. It may be necessary to supply an addi-

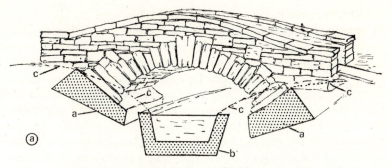

6a. Sketch of stone bridge in double perspective:
a. Concrete foundations   b. Stream in section
c. Masking with soil for planting

6b. Wooden former on which to build an arch

tional curved former between the outside ones. The formers
should be set on flat stones which can be worked out after the
bridge is built and so release the pressure and enable the formers
to be removed without disturbing the stonework.

Foundations for the arch must be adequate and must be in firm,
undisturbed ground so that there is no possibility of any give, and
consequent weakening and possible collapse of the arch.

These foundations should be below ground level, out of sight
when the job is finished. Reinforced concrete 9–12in. thick, and
finished so that the face towards the bridge is inclined at the same
angle as a radius of the arch at that point, is the best foundation
when the width of the arch is 4ft. or so.

For a lesser arch, flagstones of two or three thicknesses, set at the
correct angle and bedded with cement, should be adequate. When

the stream is still to be constructed and it has been decided where to have such a bridge I have used a method which has worked very well—I think it is about 50 years since I made my first stone bridge by this method, and it was standing as well as ever when last I saw it some 10 years ago. Having decided on the position of the stream, and its level, holes are excavated either side for the foundations, the excavated soil is thrown into the middle where the arch is to be and soil from the proposed stream is dug out and thrown on to the pile until there is enough heaped up and trodden down to fill the arch of the bridge, and a foot or so wider than the width of the bridge, either side. The heap is then carefully moulded to the required curve, beating down and adding more soil until quite firm and true. The foundations are then constructed, and the stone arch commenced from both ends, always setting the stones with their lengths along a radius of the arch, if necessary using thin stone wedges to achieve this, and jointing with cement mortar. When the centre of the arch is reached, a selected key stone is fitted to join the two half-spans neatly and firmly. Both sides of the bridge are built at the same time, and the space between the sides, also, which the path is to follow. When the keystones are in position the whole work between the two sides should be grouted with cement mortar, sufficient to fill any gaps between the stones.

When this has set, the soil supporting the arch can be dug out and taken away at any time, before or after building on the side-wall of the bridge. The side-walls may be any convenient thickness, but not less than 9in. The path over the bridge may be brought up to the required level with broken stone laced with cement mortar, and finished off with crazy paving, cobbles set in cement, or in any other fashion to taste, to provide a good walking surface. The way the stream is managed under the bridge gives great scope to the designer; it may run quietly through the arch, or a fall into a pool may be arranged, or turbulent rapids, depending on the volume of water available. It is a good idea to have a planting space between the stream and the bridge where dwarf ferns can be planted—6in. of width would be sufficient. When the work is completed and settled down, such a structure made by oneself will always be a great source of pleasure.

Of course the types of bridge described are for the informal stream, or rock and stream garden. If a bridge is required for a formal design it should be made with dressed stone and probably the services of an experienced stonemason will be required—there are still one or two left. Sometimes it is possible to obtain quantities of good squared building stone where demolition work is being carried on, and this will already have the patina of age so desirable for garden work. Of course there are numerous kinds of reconstituted stone on the market, cast in a variety of sizes so that it is possible to vary the courses while building, and so avoid the monotony of uniform courses. When an adjacent dwelling has been made with reconstituted stone, often used in new houses, it may even be desirable to use similar material for formal garden building. Anyone with a 'good eye' who can use a spirit level and plumb-line should be able to construct garden walls and so on with such artificial stone, but the arch of a bridge would require carefully shaped stone of wedge shape, made to suit the radius of the particular arch. It is essential for the two sides of the bridge to be built of carefully shaped stone for appearances' sake, but the building between the two faces may be constructed with any suitable stone wedged and cemented so that the faces of the stones coincide with the radii of the arch. As before, the path area may be levelled up with broken stone and concrete, and finished off with any suitable surface.

7. Method of terminating pool against terrace wall

It is but rarely that such a bridge will be included in a formal garden design, but a modification is sometimes used where a formal pool is built against a terrace wall. In this case, the end of a formal pool adjacent to the terrace wall may be made with a semi-circular end projecting under the terrace, which is supported by an arch built in the form of a quarter sphere over the end of the pool. Usually the stones are built in ever-widening courses from the apex of the semicircular end of the pool. The keystone in the centre of the arch may be carved in the form of an animal mask or similar concept, with a jet of water arranged to play from the jaws thereof, falling into the pool and thereby introducing movement into the design. There are such keystones to be had from the suppliers of garden sculpture, but it is rather fun to have a go at carving out such a feature oneself, when one has sufficient time. A suitable stone, a few hard-steel chisels kept sharp, and a lot of patience and perhaps a pair of goggles, and there is a job which will keep one busy creating something which may be a great source of satisfaction for years. A hole for water may be drilled with a cold chisel, turning it with every blow, taking it easy. Too much haste or too hearty blows may split the stone.

4

Pumps, Lighting, and Heated Pools

THE SELECTION AND INSTALLATION OF ELECTRIC PUMPS

When it is planned to introduce moving water into the water garden, whether in the form of waterfalls and streams or by fountain jets, spouting figures and so forth, it will be necessary to install an electric centrifugal pump of some kind. Apart from the certainty that the water authority would not allow the use of mains water for garden display when the water runs to waste, such water would be too cold for the successful cultivation of water plants. When the same water is used over and over again through a pump the temperature keeps up—at any rate when the display is concerned with streams and falls. An ambitious display of fountain jets results in rapid cooling of the water through evaporation from the thousands of tiny droplets, and this effect is detrimental to the growth of water plants.

Today there are available a large number of different pumps for the amateur pool owner. These may be separated into two main types, the submersible pumps and the surface models. The type recommended depends on the scale of the garden in which they are to be used. For the smaller pools up to 60sq. ft. in area, fibre-glass pools and the like, submersible pumps are admirable. They are very easy to install, since they merely require a level support within the pool well below the water surface. The pipe leading from the pump to the topmost part of the stream should be in one piece, preferably of alkathene, laid in a trench about a foot deep, curving in one sweep with no sharp bends to the outlet. Any sharp bends, stopcocks and unnecessary bends create pipe friction and reduce the flow.

The waterproof lead for the electric supply is usually sealed into the pump and is long enough to lead well outside the pool where it is connected with a waterproof fitting to the lead from the mains. This lead must be protected from any possible damage in some way, either by metal tubing or tiles laid over it so that it cannot be cut with garden tools, and should incorporate a switch at the source in the house or under cover. Here it cannot be stressed too strongly that advice be sought from a properly qualified electrician as to the safety of the proposed installation, and to discover any local bye-laws governing the use and installation of such apparatus. The type of cable may be specified in regulations and it may be obligatory to bury the cable a prescribed depth with a specified form of protection. The submersible pump should be one of the best quality, fully guaranteed and, furthermore, checked by your electrician friend.

Apart from the real danger to life through using substandard and possibly faulty equipment, all kinds of mysterious happenings can occur when electric current strays from its designed path. Amongst other experiences I have had when investigating faulty wiring were, getting shocks from greenhouse benches when lifting plants therefrom, and even more so when filling a metal watering-can from a greenhouse tank. One rather shattering experience brought about by electrical leaks was the continuous ringing of the telephone whenever the pump was switched on. It may seem a very simple thing to do, to join up to an electricity supply, but a little knowledge in this case can be a fatal thing.

Where a large volume of water is required for streams and falls and possible fountains, there are large-output submersible pumps which can deliver up to 3,000 gallons per hour. These pumps are too powerful for use with the smaller fibre-glass or similar-sized pools, but are useful for pools over 100sq. ft. in area. It is necessary to have streams at least 2ft. wide and deep enough to take the flow without loss, with such powerful pumps. The use of a balancing tank as described in the previous chapter is advised with such pumps.

In the larger layout, when the start of the stream and falls may be 50ft. or more from the lowest pool, a surface model pump is recommended. The pump must be housed in a waterproof but well-drained compartment made from cement rendered brick, or concrete, preferably waterproofed concrete, with either a waterproof lid or weatherproof side doors for access. The compartment must be well ventilated in order to dissipate heat from the running motor and must be big enough to contain the pump, any stop-cocks or branches for fountains, etc., and for suction and delivery pipes to lead through the side walls.

The pump chamber should be sited as close to the pool as practicable so as to keep the suction pipe as short as possible. At the same time the pump chamber should be so placed that it can be hidden from view while easy of access. Alkathene pipe should be used for the suction pipe, as rubber tubing is apt to collapse under suction, and metal pipes are subject to corrosion. If it is convenient to install the pump chamber below the pond level, a pipe brought through the pond wall to the pump will eliminate the need for a foot-valve, but of course a strainer must be fitted to prevent any pond debris getting into the pump and perhaps blocking it. When the suction pipe and pump are below water level the pipe should be joined to the pump via a stopcock to prevent accidental flooding of the pump chamber. When the pump is housed above water level the suction pipe must be fitted with a foot-valve and strainer combined, and the latter must be fixed in a vertical position if it is to work properly. Without a foot-valve, when the pump is switched off, the pump and pipes will empty themselves into the pool and the system will require priming before the pump can function again. The pump selected should have a motor of the induction type. This type is quieter and will run a very long time without needing attention. Pump motors using brushes require frequent attention, particularly when not running under full load. Such pumps running without a full load will work too fast and burn out brushes in a short time.

The vertical height from the pump to the top of the stream system is termed the 'head', and the amount of head governs the amount of flow. The requisite figures are supplied with each pump by the makers. For instance a pump which delivers 700 gallons at a 5-ft. head will deliver only 400 gallons at a 15-ft. head. When a pump is not working at full load it is possible to create an artificial head by restricting the bore of the pipe in some way, say by introducing a stopcock. By turning the stopcock to restrict the flow the motor is given more work to do, as though the head were much higher. The vertical height of the suction side, from foot-valve to pump, should not exceed 5ft., preferably less. In fact, in the case of the smaller pumps, a suction height below 5ft. is essential. Of course, in the case of submersible pumps there is no suction lift, the water being drawn direct into the pump, and the amount of flow will be determined by the head alone. When it is planned to work one or more fountain jets as well as a stream, each outlet should have a separate feed led through a branch and stopcock to the pump. By adjusting the flow through each stopcock, the volume of water from each outlet can be controlled so as to get the best effect from each outlet. It will be necessary to purchase a pump which will be large enough to deliver enough flow to work all the jets or other outlets satisfactorily.

In the winter months, if the pump is in such a position that it might be affected with frost damage, it is advisable to detach the pump and store it in a frost-proof shed until it is wanted again. At the same time the opportunity should be taken to have any necessary servicing carried out, cleaning filters and foot-valves, and flushing out any sediment which may have collected in pipes, so that a good start may be made in the following summer. If desired, a pool heater could be run from the same electricity supply. Such heaters are intended to be used only during frosty weather to keep open a small area so that oxygen can diffuse into the water and noxious gases may escape. When a quantity of dead leaves and other organic waste has been allowed to collect in the pool, bacterial action caused thereby uses up the oxygen and releases poisonous gases harmful to fish. When the pool is frozen over these gases accumulate and may reach such a concentration that they poison fish and vegetation in the water. These heaters are not intended to heat the entire pool, but merely to keep a small surface area free of ice. It is better to use one of these rather than to break up the ice with a hammer. The shock of hammer blows is transmitted through the water and may injure fish fatally. Floating wood or polystyrene blocks may keep the water free of ice in their neighbourhood if they are moved about, but rather than subject the fish to violent shocks, it is better to allow the pool to freeze over. If the pool is deep enough there will always be unfrozen depths where the fish can exist in a semi-dormant state.

Perhaps it would be as well to reiterate here—always take professional advice when installing electrical apparatus out of doors.

EMPTYING THE POOL

The problem of emptying a pool is easily solved if there is lower ground within easy reach of a hosepipe. It is just a matter of starting a syphon by placing one end of the hose in the pool within an inch or so of the bottom, taking the other end of the hose to the lowest ground available and, if one has good lungs, sucking the pipe until the water starts running. Often it starts quite suddenly and one gets a mouthful of pond water. I have suffered this many times even from old pools and cannot say that I have had any ill effects—possibly pond-water vitamins are beneficial. A less drastic method of starting a syphon is to fill the hose with water either from a can or by gradually coiling the pipe into the pool until it is quite full. In either event one end of the pipe is placed in the pool, the other end, being kept stopped firmly with a cork or thumb, is transferred to the low area when the water is released and, provided that there are no airlocks, all will be well. It is advisable to have a companion to watch that the end in the pool does not rise above the water while the pipe is being moved. If it does the syphon will be lost and one has to start again. On balance the personal suction method is the least trouble. When siphoning from an established pool, the end of the pipe should have some kind of filter over it to prevent any debris, small watersnails or fish getting down the pipe. A rose from a watering-can makes a useful sieve.

If there is an electric pump installed it is fairly simple to attach a hose to the outlet side and lead the hose to a drain or other desired spot, set the pump running and the pool will soon empty. The pump should not be allowed to run dry or it may be damaged. Complete the emptying by siphon or bailing. Bailing a full pond is a most laborious business, and after carrying the buckets away a few times, the journeys tend to get shorter and shorter, until one simply throws the water around outside the pool, creating an unholy mess. Incidentally, the 18×9 ft. pool described earlier would hold 3,000 gallons, or 1,500 bucketfuls.

Alternatively a drain may be built into the pool and led away to enter an existing drain or to a 'soakaway'. There are several methods of arranging such a drain; the most satisfactory is to fit a pipe vertically in a corner of the pool so that its open end is level with the full pool, in which position the pipe acts as an overflow. The bottom of the pipe is screwed into an 'elbow' which is itself attached to a pipe taken through the pool wall at the lowest part of the side and led to a drain. When the vertical pipe is un-

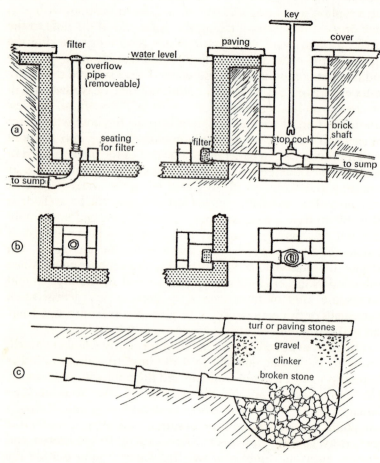

8a. Section concrete formal pool showing drainage methods
8b. Same in plan
8c. Method of draining to 'soakaway'

screwed, a wire gauze or perforated zinc filter is put over the elbow to prevent matter from the pool clogging the pipe. The pipe should be stainless steel or plastic, to prevent any poisonous matter being formed by acids in the pond water.

More elaborate, a permanently open pipe with filter is led through the pool wall into a drain, with a stopcock fitted to the pipe at some convenient point. A brick-lined chamber is built up to the surface from the stopcock and masked with a stone flag. A removable, long-shanked key is used to open the cock to allow the water to drain away.

It is unlikely that the pool need be emptied more than once in one or two years, in fact the less interference there is with an established pool which is well matured, the better. A well-balanced pool with mature water takes time to achieve but once established, plant and animal life will balance each other in a natural system which is upset by frequent interference. If plants and animal life are quite healthy leave well alone. The most likely cause of trouble is the accumulation of autumn leaves in the pool and this should be prevented as described earlier on p. 13. Needless feeding of fish—which can well look after themselves in an established pool—also can cause dangerous conditions through rotting of excess food. A pool meant for growing plants needs no fancy coloured surfacing of walls or floor, and such whimsies should be confined to swimming pools and possibly patio water gardens with fountains where plants are not necessary adjuncts. Interference with an established pool by preoccupation with maintaining spotless surfaces can lead to trouble.

Before emptying a pool, one should have at hand suitable containers in which fish may be kept during the operation. The fish are caught most easily when the water level is getting low. Remember that fish require oxygen, and therefore containers should be large enough to hold enough water for the comfort of the fish involved. The minimum volume of water is often rated as 1 gallon per inch of fish, though the surface area of the container is the more important. If some form of aeration can be supplied, a greater number of fish can be supported in otherwise inadequate containers. The fish should be returned to the pool as soon as possible after it is refilled, taking care to check that the water temperature is the same as that in the containers, for fish are very sensitive to sudden changes of temperature.

The containers should be kept in the shade or protected from direct sunlight in some way, for too bright light and too warm water cause great distress to coldwater fish. The containers should be covered with netting to prevent fish jumping out and cats fishing in.

UNDERWATER ILLUMINATION

While the pond-owner who is interested primarily in growing aquatic plants will no doubt regard underwater illumination as a form of gimmicry, many enthusiasts will wish to experience watching the beauty of the evolutions of brightly coloured fish and the grace of water plants by the glow of hidden lighting below the surface. There is no doubt that the most fascinating and fairy-like effects can be had by this means—the whole pool appears to glow, most of the light being reflected back into the water from the under-surface. The effectiveness of the light depends on the clarity of the water, and the frequent cleaning of the light source, for minute vegetative growth will coat the lamps or their covers in due course.

The safest method is to have plate-glass panels set in the pond walls, and this presupposes solid construction of the latter. Behind the panels suitable lamps are fitted in a watertight compartment to which access must be provided for servicing. These panels should be fixed near the surface, not more than 6in. down, and light should be prevented from shining upwards by a ledge or hood the length of the panel and about 6in. wide. Nowadays, waterproof lamps and fittings can be obtained, and these can be placed at strategic points below the surface. There are also such whimsies as floating lights masked by artificial water-lily leaves.

It cannot be urged too strongly that any such installations should not be attempted without the supervision of an expert, fully qualified electrician, and every precaution taken to avoid damage to cables. These should be checked regularly for signs of damage.

The use of floodlights to illuminate the water garden as a whole is frequently adopted in public gardens, and there is no reason why the amateur should not enjoy such lighting if he so wishes. It is simply a matter of carefully siting lamps so that they do not detract from the daylight view, while at the same time giving adequate illumination. The results do not compare with the almost magic beauty of underwater illumination. Installing coloured lights to illuminate fountains at night is another development sometimes seen in public gardens, and they could no doubt be an attractive feature in formal patio gardens. There are small models available which could be used in the 'home extension' with good effect. However, these decorative gadgets are rather outside the scope of a gardening book.

It is recommended that underwater lighting should not be left on all night, but just turned on for an evening stroll round the garden or when entertaining friends. Continuous lighting has a tendency to encourage attenuated growth of the submerged aquatics and also advertises the pool and its fishy denizens to the neighbourhood's cats, who will welcome such aids to fishing expeditions.

POOLS FOR TROPICAL WATER-LILIES

The number of species and hybrids of the tropical water-lilies is very great; every year new varieties are being produced, particularly in the United States of America. Where there is a warm greenhouse available, there is little problem in growing a selection of these very beautiful plants, but in the open in this country it is a real gamble trying to grow these colourful plants. In fact, unless the pool can be built in a particularly sheltered position, open to the south and in an area of high sunshine record, it is questionable whether it is worthwhile going to the trouble involved in attempting to grow them in the open .These water-lilies were grown very successfully in the old formal pool near the laboratories at the Royal Horticultural Society's Garden at Wisley, and no doubt many readers will be familiar with this example.

The construction of pools for growing the tropical water-lilies out of doors in this country must be such that some form of heating system can be introduced into the tanks. Far the most economical method is by means of hot-water pipes, led from an existing hot-water system from an adjacent greenhouse or household heating installation, and this means that the pond walls should be of concrete, brickwork or masonry. The pool should be sunk into the ground to water level to reduce heat losses through the walls, and the pipes should be led below ground, lagged very efficiently to prevent heat losses en route, and of course taken the shortest possible way from the boiler. Pipes should be of cast iron or stainless steel, since other materials might generate harmful corrosion products under water. In a moderate-sized pool, say of 60 sq. ft. area, a single line of pipes arranged round the sides of the pool near the bottom should be adequate, but in a larger pool a grid of pipes probably would be necessary. In order to thrive, tropical water-lilies require a temperature of 70 °F. (21 °C.) from early March until they begin to die down in autumn, when usually they are removed from the pool and put into store, as described later (p. 68).

Some assistance may be given in the early months by covering the pool with a removable framework bearing glass or plastic framelights. This would help to maintain the temperature which could be lowered dangerously by cold winds. A suggestion made to me that such pools be covered with plastic 'bubble' houses seems to me to be out of place in a garden intended as a place of beauty. Admirable as such structures may be in commercial establishments, they have an appearance reminiscent of the distended entrails of some stranded leviathan from the deep.

Electric heating of open-air pools, unless very small, is hardly practicable unless expense is not a consideration. Experiments with electrically heated open-air swimming pools have been carried out and, while I have not been able to obtain any details of costs, I understand that these ruled out the method. Cold moving air in contact with the water absorbs the heat continuously, and in the not unlikely event of power cuts at a time when the heat is needed most, a situation disastrous to the water-lilies might arise. Such a situation, after paying for weeks of electric power would be extremely annoying, to put it mildly.

On the other hand, tropical water-lilies do not need a great depth of water, 15 in. is adequate over the crown, and such shallow pools heat up more quickly than the deeper ones required for the hardy water-lilies. If electric heating is employed, any method of pool construction could be used as there would be no heavy pipes to support. A series of immersion heaters could have their leads led over the pool edges, suitably hidden from view. Such immersion heaters must be housed in glass or non-corrosive containers not affected by acid or alkaline water.

There is another method of electric heating by means of plastic-covered wires which could be led around the lower parts of the tank, in such a way that they were evenly distributed without being in a position where they might easily be damaged by subse-

1. *Hemerocallis* 'Jake Russel'. The Day-lilies are splendid subjects for waterside planting. There is a wide range of cultivars which have a prolonged flowering period, in all shades from pale cream to deep red

Photograph by Ernest Crowson

2. Formal pool at Walpole House, Chiswick. Contrasting erect iris foliage with quiet horizontal setting, and floating water-lilies
Photograph by Ernest Crowson

3. A small pool, recently planted and beginning to show promise of a charming feature for a small garden
Photograph by Ernest Crowson

4. Water-lilies at Chittenden House, Kent. The leaves contrast beautifully with the upright background, but the water-lilies themselves are in need of division and replanting

Photograph by Ernest Crowson

5. Rock Pool at Wisley. All concrete work is masked by rock and plantings of ferns and waterside plants. The dwarf bearded iris requires fairly dry soil, but looks well near the water

Photograph by Ernest Crowson

6. *Primula rosea*. Thriving in a pondside moist bed where the roots can reach water, the intense cerise flowers respond to April sunshine. Later the lysichitum foliage will shade the foliage from the summer sun

Photograph by Ernest Crowson

7. *Gunnera manicata*. The young foliage and flower spike in early May. Later the gunneras grow into huge specimens up to 12ft. high; each immense leaf can shelter five or six people

Photograph by H. Smith

8. *Adiantum pedatum*. This charming North American fern is absolutely hardy, but must be given a shady position   *Photograph by H. Smith*

9. *Nymphaea* 'Charles de Meurville'. A strong grower suitable for the larger pool   *Photograph by H. Smith*

quent operations in the pool. Whichever method is used, the heating should be controlled by a thermostat. The latter must be rated to control the maximum wattage required without overloading. Here it is as well to warn users under no circumstances to switch on underwater heating devices, unless they are totally immersed in water, otherwise they are liable to burn out in a short time.

It is almost impossible to forecast heating costs for the outdoor pool as the weather conditions are so variable, and the rates of cooling vary from tank to tank according to their capacity and surroundings. The smaller tanks cool more rapidly than larger ones in similar surroundings. Incidentally, the foliage of tropical water-lilies tends to spread widely in very shallow water but in any case the flowers stand well clear of the surface.

In a warm greenhouse where the temperature is kept up to 70°F. (21 °C.), there will be no need for supplementary heating. It is quite an advantage to have raised pools indoors as they will warm up more quickly than those sunk in the ground, and of course there will be no problems of building to resist ice pressure. Raised tanks should be of concrete, brickwork or masonry with a suitable coping on which one may sit and enjoy the flowers which often are strongly scented. Where there is not room for a nice-sized pool tropical water-lilies can be grown quite well in tubs or half-casks, preferably not less than 2ft. in diameter, on account of the spreading habit of the foliage. Any other containers of suitable size may be used, provided that they have been perfectly cleaned and free of all traces of former, possibly injurious, contents.

In the unheated greenhouse or in one which is not kept at tropical temperature some means must be found to keep the pool temperature up to 70 °F. (21 °C.), especially in the earlier months of the year. In summer, sun heat may be enough to keep up the temperature during the day, but during the night supplementary heating will be required, and this may be obtained economically by using off-peak heating under the 'white meter' supply system, but earlier in the year continuous heating will be necessary. If 250-watt heaters are used, three will be required to each 100 gallons of water in a pool within an unheated house. In a house which can be kept at a minimum temperature of 50 °F. (10 °C.), a small tank or tub holding 20 gallons would require about 70 watts, a 40-gallon tank about 115 watts, and a 120-gallon tank about 240 watts to maintain the requisite temperature of 70 °F. (21 °C.), so it is evident that the

E

larger tanks require less wattage per gallon than the smaller ones.

If for any reason the electricity supply fails, the cooling rate depends on the temperature of the surrounding air; pools whose water level is below that of the surrounding ground cool more slowly than the raised pool. Electricity cuts during the summer months seldom last long enough to cause a disastrous fall in temperature, in midwinter the water-lily tubers should be in store as described later, and are therefore unaffected by such troubles. If the tubers are left undisturbed in their tanks during the dormant season they will survive occasional drops in temperature to as low as 50 °F. (10 °C.) if these occasions are not prolonged, but once growth is active, temperatures must be maintained at the correct level.

Direct heating of raised pools by gas or oil burners has been employed in the past, but is not recommended. With such equipment there is a grave risk of incomplete combustion with the resulting poisonous atmosphere. Such pools are built generally of galvanized iron, on a grid of girders under which is installed the heating apparatus, either a grid of gas jets or a series of oil burners, all of which require constant supervision. Such tanks must be coated internally with a suitable paint, containing no injurious materials and which will remain in good condition over long periods. The external walls could be masked with brick or stonework. When it is wished to employ such forms of heating it is better to use it to heat hot water in a boiler and transfer the heat to the lily pool by means of hot-water pipes. The heating unit should be kept in a separate compartment which can be ventilated without impairing the heating efficiency of the pipe system.

The Care of Hardy and Tender Aquatic Plants

The best time for planting hardy aquatic plants of all kinds depends to a great extent on the weather, and to a lesser extent on location. Generally the best months are May and June; in the south April may be warm enough, though a cold, late spring may make it advisable to delay two or three weeks. Outdoor pools begin to warm up as the spring sunshine increases and the days lengthen. After midsummer's day, day length gradually diminishes and when July arrives, the best planting time has passed. August is too late for newly planted water-lilies to establish themselves sufficiently to survive the approaching colder weather, though marginal aquatics may be planted then with every expectancy of success. Submerged aquatics and oxygenators such as elodea and myriophyllum may be moved any time between May and August and then will establish themselves sufficiently to survive the winter.

Between August and the following April, it is almost always fatal to move aquatic plants, unless it is a matter of moving containers complete with soil and plants whose roots are still confined within the container, to another pool. Planting crates containing plants which have extended their roots beyond the confines of their containers should be left severely alone during this period of autumn, winter, and early spring. When water-lilies are moved at any time any roots which are damaged will rot, and new roots must be formed before the plants can be expected to grow. The leaves of water-lilies which have just been purchased often die off, but in the correct planting period new leaves soon appear and all will be well—one hopes.

The best medium in which to plant all water plants is a good quality heavy loam preferably prepared by stacking the turf from a good meadow in the open some six months previously. Water-lilies are gross feeders, and will appreciate extra nourishment. If cow manure is available the turf should be stacked with a layer 1in. thick of cow manure between every two layers of turf or every 6in., until the stack is 3 or 4ft. high, and 5 or 6ft. square. The heap should be turned two or three times during the six months required. A second heap without manure should be prepared with which to surface the manured loam, to prevent the latter coming into contact with the water, for manured loam always causes active growth of algae. In the absence of cow manure use bonemeal, 2oz. to each square yard of turf, as it is stacked. Other animal manures are quite unsuitable or even dangerous—there is some special virtue in cowdung which endears it to all horticulturists.

If it has not been possible to prepare a turf stack, some good quality top-spit loam from a meadow should be well broken up, and rubbed through a $\frac{1}{2}$-in. sieve, removing all roots and stones, until the required quantity is obtained, a 3-in. potful of bonemeal being mixed with each bushel of loam. This will make a good planting medium. Of course, the stacked loam also should be well sieved before use. Sand, gravel and stone chips are useless in the rooting medium though some people use stone chips to surface the loam to prevent its disturbance by fish rooting around. Leafmould and peat, and in fact any vegetable matter, is actively injurious if it is incorporated in water-lily compost, however attractive it may seem. The decay of such material under water creates acid conditions harmful to plants and fish alike. At all costs do not be tempted to use mud from natural ponds, ditches or streams under the mistaken impression that such material might be just what the plants need. Such material almost always is leached of all nutriment and furthermore is likely to contain all manner of pests and seeds of rampageous pond weeds. However interesting it might be to the student of pond biology, it is definitely 'out' so far as the garden pool is concerned.

Having assembled the materials, the actual planting is much more quickly done. After previously draining away the water, the planting ledges, where these have been provided around the perimeter of the pool, are filled partway with the manured loam, and then topped up with 2in. of manure-free loam. If the deeper parts of the pool have been provided with planting places for water-lilies as recommended earlier (pp. 34-35), these also are filled with a 3- or 4-in. depth of manured loam and topped up with manure-free loam.

These planting places are best made with two or three courses of bricks laid without mortar to form squares or circles 2ft. in diameter, 6-9in. deep. If it is not convenient to provide squares as large as those recommended, smaller squares will keep water-lilies growing for a time, possibly two years, but the lilies will require replanting in fresh compost at least every second year. As soon as the plants start producing reduced-size foliage and flowers, it is a sign that the medium is becoming exhausted.

When the soil is in position water should be run in carefully so as not to disturb the soil and the pool left to warm up before the plants are introduced. Newly-run water from the mains is too cold for the good of the new plants, and also may contain chlorine so it is wise to have the pool ready two or three weeks before the plants arrive. The plants have already had a shock from removal from their nursery beds, and a sojourn in the post, and the further shock of too cold water will set them back further.

When the plants arrive from the nurseryman, usually towards the end of May, they are likely to be showing signs of growth and they should be planted as soon as possible. If for any reason immediate planting is not practicable the plants should be un-packed at once and placed in water in bowls, buckets or similar containers, taking care to arrange the growths in their natural positions. If the plants are not so disposed they will bend towards their natural positions and develop a permanent kink which will persist throughout the season.

Planting marginal aquatics is just a simple matter of spreading their roots in the wet loam deep enough to cover them but leaving the growing point of the shoot in view at the loam surface. Before planting, decide on their arrangement, trying to dispose the plants so that styles of growth and types of foliage contrast with one another. For instance, the glossy cordate foliage of *Calla palustris* contrasts well with the variegated spears of *Acorus calamus variegatus*; *Pontederia cordata* with *Limnanthemum peltatum*, and so forth. While the majority of marginal plants are quite happy in 3 or 4in. of soil, certain kinds, such as lysichitum and orontium need deep soil; 12in. is not too much, so special positions must be provided to accommodate such plants, when they are desired.

The more rampant marginals really are not suited for growing in a small pool, they are admirable for lakeside planting or for the very large pool where they can spread themselves without imperilling their less robust neighbours. Those plants which spread rather rapidly, such as *Typha minima*, the sagittarias, butomus, and the like, can be used in the small pool if their roots are confined in containers with solid sides and bottoms so that their creeping propensities are curbed. In time they will climb out of their containers and will need to be rehoused.

WATER-LILIES

Water-lilies should be planted with the roots spread well out in the medium, the growing point just showing at the surface. An alternative method of planting the water-lilies in an established pool is to put them in planting crates, the perforated plastic pattern is quite good—and then lower the crate into the pool, not the full depth but to a shallow part so that there is 3 or 4in. of water above the crown. When growth starts freely, the crate is gradually drawn into deeper water and left a few days, finally drawing the crate to the planned planting place. The lily roots will grow through the perforated sides and bottom, and take hold of the soil in the planting square. The reason for this procedure is to allow the water-lily to extend the leaf-stalks so that the leaves float on the water surface as soon as possible, and make use of the sunlight to manufacture food for the nourishment of the crown.

As the leaf stalks lengthen, so the plant is moved to the correct depth of water. If planted in the correct depth at once, it is a strain on the plant, and it may even fail before the leaves reach the surface. If the pool is empty when the plants arrive, the water-lilies should be firmly planted in their positions and enough water run in to cover the crowns by 3 or 4 inches. They are then left a few days for the water to warm up and growth to start, then a few more inches of water are run in, and left again to warm up, and so on until the pool is filled. This procedure may seem tedious, but it is far better to wait for the water-lilies to adjust to their new surroundings by degrees while the water warms up slowly. A pool completely filled at once will take three weeks or more to reach a genial temperature. Any marginal plants must be kept in water to the last until the pool is filled up to their planting ledges, when they may be set in their places.

To avoid disturbing soil when running in water, this should be run into a bowl of some kind which will overflow gently on to the pool bottom. Planting, by the way, should be very firm.

Instead of using more or less permanent planting squares, movable containers for water-lilies may be constructed of timber; boxes 2ft. square and 6in. deep, inside measurement, would be excellent. The bottom of the box need not be provided with holes. Such containers enable the plants to be moved around if so desired, with no risk of damage to the plants. The plastic planting crates at present available are too small for the larger water-lilies, but the smaller, less strong growing kinds will do well enough in them although they will need providing with fresh soil at least every other season. Those crates supplied for the marginal aquatics are quite satisfactory and there are several designs available. Once the plants are growing freely, they will mask the rather obvious containers. The very small ones, 3 or 4in. in diameter are suitable only for the smallest marginals, but can be used for planting oxygenators such as elodea and myriophyllum.

Actually, these oxygenators do not need planting at all, the strands are simply gathered together with their growing points to one end, and the other end is tied to a small stone or lead clip and just lowered into the water. They will soon make themselves at home and spread freely. The professional water-lily grower will cover the entire bottom of his pools with at least 6in. depth, probably more, of good loam so that his plants will grow freely and so become ready for propagation more quickly. The roots of a medium-sized water-lily after a year's growth will extend over a circle 4ft. in diameter, when there is room for it to develop.

Another method of adding water-lilies to the established pool is to make a kind of sandwich with two squares of turf, the grass having been shorn very close, with the water-lily used as a filling. The rhizome is placed on one turf with its roots spread well out and the crown just showing at the edge of the turf, then the other turf is placed over it and the whole bound together with plastic tape. The sandwich is then lowered into the pool, being careful to keep the water-lily right side up until it reaches the chosen position.

A further method is to plant the water-lily in a chip basket made from wood, not the cardboard type such as is used for market garden produce. The basket is lowered as before, in stages if the pool is deep, until finally in position. The water-lily will send its roots through the joints of the basket, into the soil, and the basket will eventually disintegrate, leaving the lily well established.

FLOATING PLANTS

Free-floating aquatics such as the frog-bit simply need dropping in the water when they will look after themselves. A word of warning. Unless there is some special reason why such floating plants as the duckweeds, or lemna spp., are required, take every care to avoid introducing them to your pool. They will grow into a solid mat completely covering the pool's surface, and cutting off all light to the underwater aquatics, oxygenators and the like, so that these become attenuated and may even die out altogether. An exception is azolla, the floating fern, a charming plant which can be removed fairly easily if it gets out of hand. I remember one of my tanks being covered solidly with this plant. Our cat leapt into the centre of the verdant carpet and disappeared in several inches of water. She emerged very bedraggled, decorated with bits of azolla and wearing a most reproachful expression.

PROPAGATION

The propagation of the majority of aquatics is just a matter of careful division in May or June, replanting the divisions in fresh soil. Certain plants such as lysichitum and orontium resent transplanting—and indeed are very difficult to extricate from the wet soil after they have been established a year or two—and they are best left to make larger and larger specimens. However, they set seed freely, and if the plants are watched carefully and the seeds secured just before they become detached from the spikes, they can be sown in shallow pans of loam standing up to their brims in water. The pans should be kept in a cold greenhouse, a sunny frame or even on a sunny window ledge, if one is allowed.

Germination usually takes place within a few weeks, the plants may be left until large enough to pot up individually or they may be kept until the following spring when they should be carefully washed out, the roots separated and the young plants lined out in a suitable pool. Naturally, the pans must never be allowed to get dry at any time.

HARDY WATER-LILIES

These seldom set seed in this country, but if they do, they should be treated in the same way. The ripe seeds dehisce and float in the water for a day before they sink. They should be secured before they disappear, and sown in shallow pans covered with an inch of water. The pans are best kept in a cool greenhouse from which frost can be excluded, in a sunny position. The seedlings are then left till the following spring, when they should be potted up individually in small pots in sterilized loam, and set in tanks just deep enough for the water to cover the pots by an inch or so. When the plants are growing freely they should be hardened off, and finally planted in shallow pools out of doors, until they are strong enough to transplant into deeper water.

In general, hardy water-lilies are propagated by dividing the crowns in May, when a plant has developed several crowns. These are carefully separated with 3 or 4in. of rhizome; the older parts of the rhizome may be thrown away. Some water-lilies produce small bulbils on the rhizome, which will eventually show leaf initials, when they may be detached and potted up in very small pots in sterilized loam, and stood in shallow tanks in a greenhouse in a sunny position. They should grow away and make nice plants for planting out the following spring. They will need careful hardening off before being put out of doors.

PLANTING THE TENDER WATER-LILIES

The tropical water-lilies must be amongst the most beautiful flowers evolved in the world. A tremendous range of hues, mostly soft clear colours, large flowers of attractive shape, the majority having exquisite perfume, and all having fascinating foliage, what more can one desire? As usual, there is one snag which may be insuperable. These tender water-lilies cannot be grown unless a water temperature of 70 °F. (21 °C.) can be maintained throughout the growing season. In fact, these plants can be grown and flowered all the year round in a warm sunny greenhouse if the temperature can be kept up to the minimum. One or two kinds can be grown at 65 °F. (18 °C.), but the majority begin to lose foliage and go dormant as soon as the water temperature drops below that recommended. Given the right conditions they are easy to grow, and may do well in the outdoor pool during a warm sunny summer.

To start these water-lilies into growth, the small tubers are potted singly in good loamy soil in March, and immersed in water in containers which will allow some 4–5in. depth above the pots. Provided the temperature does not drop, there should be signs of growth within two weeks. As soon as floating leaves are formed, it is time to move the plants to their permanent homes. Tropical water-lilies are even more gross in their appetites than the hardy ones, and each plant must have at least 4 or 5cu. ft. of good loam, which has been stacked six months with cow manure, as described for the hardy varieties (p. 68). Planting boxes 2ft. square by 1ft. deep are advised, unless it is intended to grow the tender water-lilies all the year round, for usually the tropical kinds are treated as annuals, or at any rate overwintered as dormant tubers out of water. When the transplanted plants are growing well, the depth of water, which at first should not be more than 3 or 4in. above the crown, may be increased by stages to not more than 12in., which is the deepest that these lilies require. When transplanting, every care should be taken to prevent the plants becoming dry for even a short time; the rather thin-textured foliage will suffer severely unless kept wet, and loss of foliage at this stage may well cripple the plants.

At the end of the season, the pool is allowed to cool down so that the foliage will begin to die down. When this is complete the planting boxes should be lifted out of the pool, and the tubers carefully removed and laid out in a well-ventilated place, not too cold, until the old roots and foliage have withered away and can be removed. If the plants have been grown in genial conditions, the old tuber will have formed several smaller tubers around the base. These should be separated and stored in damp sand in a container which does not dry out and one which is safe against raids by rodents. Mice are exceedingly fond of the tubers. A large glass jar with a perforated zinc lid is a good receptacle.

This should be kept in a temperature around 55 °F (13 °C.), not less, until the following March, when it is time to start the tubers into growth once more.

PROPAGATION OF THE TENDER WATER-LILIES

This habit of forming several small tubers during the growing season affords a ready means of increasing stock. The smaller tubers frequently winter better than the larger ones which sometimes rot while in store. Plants which have been grown in open unheated pools may not form tubers so if it is desired to continue growing the tender lilies new stock must be obtained the following spring. Some species of tender water-lilies are viviparous, forming young plants during the summer at the junction of leaf stalk and blade. These may be detached, potted up and grown on in shallow water into larger plants. Another method of increasing stock is to carefully remove the growths with roots from the developing tuber, when the latter will form another crown in due course, and in a good season this procedure may be repeated three or four times.

The majority of tropical water-lilies freely set seed, and also hybridize readily. When the capsule is ripe, it will dehisce into the water, and it is a good idea to detach the capsule as soon as it is seen to be ready and place it in a bowl of water. At first, the seeds will float until the buoyant membrane rots, when they will fall to the bottom of the bowl. The seed may be dried and stored, or sown immediately in sterilized loam in very shallow water maintained at about 80 °F. (27 °C.). As the seed sets best towards the end of summer, it will be necessary to keep the seedlings growing all winter in a sunny warm greenhouse kept up to at least 75 °F. (24 °C.). As soon as the seedlings form floating-leaves—the first growths are grass-like—they should be potted individually in 'thimbles' or 'thumbs', the smallest pots, and potted on as they need more room, in loam to which has been added crumbled dried cow manure (old, not fresh) and kept growing until they can be planted out in their final receptacles. Of course the seedlings must be immersed in sufficient water to cover the crowns by 2 or 3 inches.

If it is desired to experiment with hybridization, great care must be taken to exclude unwanted pollen which is sure to be floating around if many tender water-lilies are being grown. The method is to select likely looking buds and, just before they are ready to open but still closed, force open the bud and remove all the stamens with a pair of forceps. The bud is then closed and secured with a tie of soft wool near the bud tip. The pollen plant is chosen two or three days later, a few stamens removed and kept in a closed glass tube until the seed parent is ready for pollination. At this state there will be a bead of nectar in the centre of the flower. Place a stamen on the stigma and close up the flower again so that no other pollen can get in. At the same time tie a muslin bag round the flower and attach the whole to a stake and leave until ripe. Then remove the fruit to open in a basin of water. Water-lily fruits usually ripen under water, but come up to the surface to dehisce when ready. Keep a record of your crosses for future reference with dates of pollination, ripening, and subsequent developments.

The American growers are responsible for a very large number of beautiful hybrids amongst the tender water-lilies, which do particularly well in the United States of America. There are approaching 200 distinct species and hybrids listed by American nurserymen and botanic gardens, though comparatively few kinds are grown in this country in commercial establishments.

PROPAGATION OF NELUMBOS

The Lotus (*Nelumbo*) spreads by means of underground runners, and may extend 20–30ft in a season with nodes 10–12in. apart. An established plant grown in a suitable container when carefully removed and washed free of soil should provide several pieces with at least two nodes, each of which should make plants if kept warm and moist. Seed is rather tricky, the large seeds are harvested in autumn, removed from the pods and stored under water in a frost- and rodent-free place. In March the seeds should be scored with a file and sown individually in sterilized loam in 5- or 6-in. pots, and submerged in water kept at 70–75 °F. (21–24 °C.) until germination takes place. The seedlings should be transferred to their planting boxes as soon as large enough. They can be grown out of doors during the summer in this country, but are far better kept under glass, where they will make enormous, stately plants and flower much more freely. The greatest care must be taken not to injure the growing point, which will die if bruised in any way. Because of the rapid growth of the rhizomes, they are best grown in circular containers, such as half-casks, which will guide the growing point around and around. In a square container they can injure themselves trying to push through the sides.

The Hardy Water-lilies

Today a great variety of hybrid hardy water-lilies is available for the amateur grower, largely due to the skill of the late Latour-Marliac, who spent many years hybridizing the hardy species in his nurseries in the south of France. This amazing man discovered the way but kept his knowledge to himself, and no one since has been so successful in raising new cultivars.

From the gardener's point of view the species of *Nymphaea* are not so important as the hybrids, but where there is room it is at least of some interest to grow one or two species. Naturally, with such a wealth of material there is a great range of size, vigour and floriferousness. The last characteristic depends very largely on environment, but the other qualities are usually analysed into four groups, as suggested by Marliac:

Group I, or A	Very strong growers, suitable for large pools and lakes, with a surface spread 10ft. in diameter, water depth 2½–4ft.
Group II, or B	Strong growers, surface spread 5–7ft. in diameter, water depth 1½–2ft.
Group III, or C	Medium growers for small pools, surface spread 2–4ft. in diameter, water depth 1–1½ft.
Group IV, or D	Small growers for small pools, tubs, etc., surface spread 1–2ft. in diameter, depth 4–12in.

Nymphaea

N. alba. Our native water-lily, the white water-lily, bright green foliage, medium flowers, 3–4in. diameter. Flowers best in deep water; I have found them frequently in water over my head in our Lakeland tarns. A.

'Candidissima'. Possibly a hybrid between *N. alba* and *N. candida*. Large white flowers not freely produced, but a very vigorous grower. A.

'Plenissima'. Another large-flowered white. A.

rubra. Seldom seen red Swedish water-lily, said to do best in very cold water. The pink flowers age to deep red. Has been culti-vated over 100 years. A.

N. 'Albatross'. Large, pure white flowers, prominent golden-yellow stamens. The foliage, purple when young, ages to deep bronze-green. C.

N. 'Amabilis'. ('Pink Marvel'). Large, tulip-shaped stellate flowers, soft salmon-pink ageing to silvery rose, bright yellow stamens, flowers remaining open later than other cultivars. Fragrant. A, B.

N. 'Andreana'. Very large flowers, 8–10in. wide, garnet-red, shaded yellow, glossy red-blotched green foliage. C.

N. 'Arc-en-Ciel'. Notable for its variegated foliage which may be blotched with bronze, purple, white and rose. Salmon-white flowers flaked rose. B.

N. 'Arethusa'. Large, globular flowers, deep velvety crimson in the centre changing to deep rose in the outer petals. B.

N. 'Atropurpurea'. Possibly the darkest crimson, a very brilliant flower, the foliage is purple when young, ageing to green. B.

N. 'Attraction'. Large, 7–8in. garnet-red flowers ageing to rich deep red, white, rose-flaked sepals. A.

N. 'Aurora'. The small flowers open yellow, ageing orange and finally dark red, pretty miniature foliage mottled maroon. Ideal for small pools. D.

N. 'Baroness Orczy'. Pretty, cup-shaped rose-pink flowers, a medium grower. B.

N. 'Bory de Saint Vincent'. One of the newer, red-flowered hybrids, not yet appearing in catalogues.

N. 'Brakleyi Rosea'. Soft rose flowers, green foliage, a rapid grower. B.

N. candida. Small white flower with a red stigma, green foliage. A species widespread throughout N. Europe, N. Asia and also in the Himalaya. The several geographical forms are inferior to the type. D.

N. 'Carisbrookii'. Small, fragrant, rose flowers. C.

N. caroliniana. Possibly a hybrid between *N. odorata rosea* and *N. tuberosa*, found in N. America. Delicate rose-pink; yellow stamens, fragrant. Foliage robust. B, C.

'Nivea'. Very large-flowered, fragrant white. C.

'Perfecta'. Salmon-pink, fragrant flowers. B.

'Rosea'. Improved, deeper colour, and beautifully shaped flowers. B, C.

N. 'Charles de Meurville'. Very vigorous. Immense flowers the colour of Burgundy wine, up to 10in. diameter. A.

N. 'Chrysantha'. Small, reddish yellow flowers ageing to cinnabar-red, free-flowering and dwarf. D.

N. 'Colonel Welch'. Strong-growing, marbled foliage, not too free-flowering, and the stellate yellow flowers always seem slightly deformed with me. There are better varieties. A.

N. 'Colossea'. Very large, pale pink flowers all summer. A.

N. 'Comanche'. Warm rose flowers, overlaid apricot, darkening to deep red. Brilliant orange stamens, young foliage purple. C.

N. 'Comte de Bouchard'. An old cultivar, small purplish rose flowers, apricot stamens. Very free-flowering. B.

N. 'Conqueror'. Brilliant red flowers flecked white, white sepals, bright yellow stamens. Prolific bloomer. B, C.

N. 'Darwin'. Reddish flowers striped white, fragrant. B.

N. 'Dawn'. Huge, fragrant snow-white flowers, pink-edged sepals. Probably an *odorata* variety. B.

N. 'Delicata'. An old *N. candida* hybrid seldom seen nowadays; white, tulip-shaped flowers. D.

N. 'Dorothy Lamour'. A recent American cultivar. Pale yellow flowers, green foliage, striped chestnut brown. D.

N. 'Eburnea'. Small, shapely white flowers, lined with green and pink, sweetly scented. Bright green foliage. C.

N. 'Ellisiana'. Brilliant garnet-red flowers, orange stamens, dark green foliage. A very popular variety. C.

N. erecta. Small, slender white flowers held well above the water. C.

III. First class design and planting in the pool garden at Godmersham, Kent. I am not sure that the jets are necessary

IV. Nymphaea 'Escarboucle'. By far the most popular of the red water-lilies

N. 'Escarboucle'. Probably and rightly the most popular of the reds. Bright crimson-red flowers, red-tipped orange stamens, free-flowering, up to 10in. diameter in good conditions. A.

N. 'Esmeralda'. Stellate red flowers, streaked white. C.

N. 'Eucharist'. Good-sized, soft rose flowers, flaked white. C.

N. 'Eugenia de Land'. A good *odorata* cultivar. Large, stellate, rich pink fragrant flowers, standing out of the water. C.

N. 'Evangeline'. Free blooming. Stellate, opalescent flesh-pink flowers, C.

N. 'Fabiola'. Large, rich pink flowers deepening towards the centre, mahogany stamens. One of the best. B.

N. fennica. The Finnish water-lily, seldom seen, requiring very cold water to survive and flower. Small white flowers, small, bright green foliage. B, C.

N. 'Firecrest'. Deep pink flowers, fiery red stamens, and very fragrant. American. C.

N. flava (syn. *N. mexicana*). This Mexican species can be grown only in the warmer districts. The bright yellow flowers stand well out of the water, the small leaves are bright green with purple blotches, the lower sides purplish red striped black. B.

N. 'Formosa'. Soft rose flowers, deepening with age. Immense boss of yellow stamens. Flowers continuously all summer. B.

N. 'Froebelii'. Masses of small blood-red flowers, very popular for tub cultivation. C.

N. 'Fulva'. An old cultivar with coppery red flowers of thin texture, and now superseded by better varieties. C.

N. 'Galatee'. An oldish cultivar, smallish rose flowers splashed white. Purple-variegated green foliage. B.

N. 'Gladstoniana'. One of the best whites for the large pool, flowers of solid texture up to 8in. across, standing well out of the water, brilliant green foliage. A.

N. 'Gloire de Temple-sur-Lot'. Very double, chrysanthemum-like creamy white flowers, incurved, flushed pink when opening. A, B.

N. 'Gloriosa'. Large, carmine-rose flowers darkening as they age, remaining open longer than most varieties, apple-scented. Medium foliage. One of the best. B.

N. 'Goliath'. Large, tulip-shaped, long-petalled flowers of white shaded pink, contrasting with the white stamens outlined by orange-red staminodes. A lovely thing. A.

N. 'Gonnêre'. ('Crystal White'). One of my favourite water-lilies,

F

the very double, pure white flowers are held in globular form by the rich green sepals. A, B.

N. 'Graziella'. The small reddish yellow flowers lighten to canary-yellow as they age. Foliage mottled purple. C.

N. 'Hassell' (*marliacea mexicana*). Rich yellow flowers 7in. diameter, long petals, flowering better in deep water. D.

N. 'Hermine'. A profuse bloomer, small stellate white flowers. C.

N. 'Hever White'. Large, stellate, milk-white flowers, rather shyly produced. A.

N. 'Indiana'. A delicate orange-red, ageing through coppery shades to dark coppery red. Mottled foliage. B.

N. 'J. C. N. Forestier'. Large flowers, soft rose-copper deepening to dark copper-bronze, standing out of water. B.

N. 'James Brydon'. One of the finest water-lilies for medium or small pools, will stand slight shade. The cup-shaped blooms are a rich carmine-red with orange stamens. Very free-flowering. Dark purple-green foliage. B, C.

N. 'James Hudson'. This elderly cultivar has large stellate flowers of purplish crimson, outer sepals rose flushed white. Green foliage. B.

N. 'Johann Pring'. An American miniature. Deep pink flowers shading to light rose, inner stamens orange-yellow, outer ones deep pink. D.

N. 'Lactea'. An old variety. Medium pinkish flowers ageing to milk-white, bright green sepals. B.

N. 'Laydekeri'. Under this name we have a group of smallish growing plants, raised by Marliac, all splendid plants for the smaller pool, and for tub cultivation, and as a rule very free flowering. A 'must' for the small garden.

'Fulgens'. Glowing amaranth-crimson, rose-flushed white sepals, fiery red stamens. Dark green foliage. C, D.

'Lilacea'. Soft rosy lilac, fragrant blooms, yellow stamens. The scent resembles that of a tea rose. C, D.

'Purpurata'. One of the freest flowering water-lilies, well established plants may carry dozens of flowers of rich rosy crimson, sometimes flecked white. C.

'Rosea'. Unfortunately, this, the loveliest of the Laydekeri group, is a weak grower. I kept it going throughout the last war, but lost it a few years ago and now it seems to have been lost everywhere. Perfect cup-shaped, deep rose, fragrant flowers. C, D.

N. 'Leviathan'. Strong growing, soft pink, fragrant. A.

N. 'Livingstone'. Long-petalled bright red tulip-like flowers, flaked with white. Stamens mahogany-red. C.

N. 'Loose'. A fine American cultivar. Pure white stellate flowers up to 7in. diameter, standing a foot above the water, resembling a 'tropical'. Scented. B, C.

N. 'Louise'. A new American introduction, a hybrid between 'Mrs C. W. Thomas' and 'Escarboucle', producing medium-sized, cup-shaped blooms of deepest clear vermilion-red with conspicuous yellow stamens. Foliage clear green. B, C.

N. 'Lucida'. Rosy vermilion flowers deepening towards the centre. Foliage variegated with purple. B.

N. 'Lusitania'. A strong grower with deep rose flowers, bright mahogany stamens. New foliage purple, ageing to green. A.

N. 'Lustrous'. A fine American cultivar. Opalescent rose-pink blooms, very free. Compact habit. Sets seed well. B, C.

N. 'Marguerite Laplace'. Very fine, its deep rose, open flowers appear continuously all summer. Purplish foliage. A, B.

N. 'Mme Bory Latour Marliac'. Comparatively recent introduction, a medium grower with pale pink flowers. C.

N. 'Mme de Bonseigneur'. Small pink flowers, striped dark pink and red. C.

N. 'Mme Julien Chifflot'. A strong grower. The immense rich pink flowers are stellate, with rich yellow stamens and often exceed 10in. diameter. A.

N. 'Mme Maurice Laydeker'. Medium-sized globular, rich cherry-red flowers. This beautiful cultivar was doing very well until my wife's geese found them! Alas, that finished them. B.

N. 'Mme P. Cazeneuve'. Large, purplish rose cup-shaped flowers standing well out of the water. Very free flowering. C.

N. 'Mme Wilfron Gonnêre'. A fine water-lily. The large, very double pink flowers deepen towards the centre. Sepals white. B.

N. Marliacea Hybrids. This is a group of some of the best of M. Marliac's hybrids, all of good form and habit.

    'Albida'. Fine massive flowers with good fragrance. Waxy white petals, rich yellow stamens and bright green foliage. A, B.

    'Carnea'. Flowers white, flushed pink, produced freely. The colour improves when the plants are well established. Strong growing. A, B.

'Chromatella'. One of the most popular, the soft yellow flowers often approach 6in. across. They are produced very freely. The foliage is mottled handsomely, the plants spread quickly and adapt themselves to varying depths. B.

'Flammea'. The amaranth-red flowers are flecked with white, the foliage is mottled chestnut on green. C.

'Rosea'. One of the best for cutting, the flowers are fragrant and last well. Deep rose deepening towards the centre, the flowers do not show full colour until the plants are well established. A, B.

'Rubra punctata'. Globular, deep rosy carmine flowers. B.

N. 'Mary Exquisita. Large-flowered, beautiful soft rose-pink flowers with a delicious perfume. Free flowering. B.

N. 'Mary Patricia'. Continuous blooming. Large cup-shaped, peach-blossom-pink flowers. C.

N. 'Masaniello'. Large, sweet-scented peony-shaped flowers, pink flaked carmine. Stamens orange-yellow. The flowers stand well out of the water. B.

N. 'Maurice Laydeker'. Small deep rose flowers. Being of poor constitution it is seldom grown today. C.

N. 'Meteor'. Red flowers streaked with white. Seldom grown now. B.

N. 'Moorei'. An Australian cultivar very similar to N. *marliacea* 'Chromatella', having canary-yellow flowers, bright yellow stamens, and foliage mottled brown. A good grower. B.

N. 'Mrs C. W. Thomas'. A fine American hybrid recently introduced, said to be the most delicately beautiful water-lily yet produced. Fragrant, shell-pink flowers, freely borne. B.

N. 'Mrs Richmond'. This very-free flowering plant has very large globular, deep pink flowers deepening in colour towards the centre. B.

N. 'Murillo'. Broad-petalled, stellate flowers with deep rose petals shaded white at their edges. The flowers float flat on the water. B.

N. 'Neptune'. One of the 'musts'. Stellate, deep rosy crimson flowers, with rosy stamens. B.

N. 'Newton'. Brilliant, vermilion-rose stellate flowers standing well out of the water. Stamens rose, foliage purple when young. B.

N. *nitida*. A Siberian species closely resembling N. *odorata* except that the rootstock is vertical instead of horizontal.

N. 'Nobilissima'. Resembling but inferior to 'Newton'. B.

N. 'Odalisque'. The rose flowers age to shell-pink, the stamens are golden. The flowers stand up well above the water. B, C.

N. odorata. A fine North American species much used in the production of hybrids, mostly fragrant. *N. odorata* itself has medium, pure white cup-shaped blooms with a strong perfume; the bright green foliage is characteristic. *N. odorata* hybrids are usually very prolific. B.

'Alba'. An improved form.

'Exquisita'. Brilliant rosy carmine, smallish flowers. C, D.

gigantea. Large, pure white flowers. This form from south-east America does best in deep water. A.

'Helen Fowler'. The finest in this section, the large 9in. blooms are a lovely deep rose, strongly scented. B, C.

'Jessieana'. Another fine pink-flowered form. B, C.

'Luciana'. Small, deep rich rose, scented, stellate flowers which, when well established, stand well out of the water. D.

minor. North America. Half the size of the type, this form does well in a wide range of depths. Very sweet. D.

floribus roseis. Similar, the outer petals tinged pink. C.

rosea. Cape Cod water-lily. Intense rose-pink flowers deepening in hue towards the centre, yellow stamens. The purplish green foliage sets off the flowers well. Perhaps the most attractively perfumed of any water-lily. B, C.

'Prolifera'. A particularly free-flowering form. B.

'Sulphurea' (*odorata* × *flava*). The deep yellow flowers stand well above water, the foliage is blotched with chocolate. Fine for small pools. C.

'Grandiflora'. A larger flowered form. C.

'Turicensis'. Medium grower, soft rose flowers. B, C.

'Wm. B. Shaw'. The delicate pink flowers are of good size and shape, and may be flushed apricot in a good summer. B, C.

N. 'Paul Hariot'. This old cultivar is very popular on account of the changing colours. Opening a soft apricot, it passes through orange-pink to quite a deep red on the third day. Maroon spotted foliage. Free flowering. C, D.

N. 'Phoebus'. The blooms open yellow, striped red, and age to a coppery red. Fiery orange stamens. Purple blotched foliage makes this a most attractive plant. C.

N. 'Phoenix'. Bright red blooms, striped white. Green foliage. C.

N. 'Picciola'. Immense, amaranth-crimson blooms, abundantly produced. A splendid cultivar. A.

N. 'Pink Opal'. The stellate flowers are a delightful coral-pink, strongly perfumed, and they stand well above the water. Excellent for cutting. C.

N. 'Princess Elizabeth'. Free-flowering hybrid, peach-pink flowers deepening and intensifying as the flower ages. C.

N. 'Punctata'. Rosy lilac flowers spotted carmine. D.

N. pygmaea alba. Although at one time considered synonymous with *N. tetragona*, the two plants are quite distinct in cultivation and this form is definitely hardier than the latter. Tiny white flowers, 1½in. across, bright green foliage. Sets seed well. Will do well in bulb bowls and other small containers. D.

    'Helvola'. This charming dwarf has soft sulphur flowers and prettily marbled leaves. D.

    'Hyperion'. Rather larger than the preceding and having amaranth-red blooms. Very free flowering. D.

    'Rubra'. The largest of this section, the blooms open a warm rose, and age to a deep garnet-red, and it flowers continuously. It is a scarce plant. C, D.

    'Rubis'. Pomegranate-red, streaked white. Said to be the smallest and most floriferous pygmy by the raiser, M. Marliac. I have not seen this cultivar. D.

N. 'Radiance'. American. The incurved petals are an iridescent shell-pink, deepening in the centre. The flowers frequently exceed 7in. diameter. B.

N. 'Rembrandt'. Handsome, wine-red flowers, maturing currant-red. A vigorous grower. B.

N. 'René Gerard'. Immense stellate flowers, rich rose flaked with crimson. A very free flowering variety. B.

N. 'Robinsoniana'. An old cultivar which still stands out, the medium-sized flowers are bright orange-red, overlaid yellow and rose, with vivid orange stamens. The foliage is spotted maroon and the flowers remain open nine hours a day. C.

N. 'Rose Arey'. Definitely a 'must'. The stellate flowers are of a uniform rich pink, sweetly fragrant and slightly incurved. B, C.

N. 'Rose Magnolia'. American cultivar. Flesh-pink flowers standing well out of the water. A delightful plant. B.

N. 'Rose Nymphe'. One of the most valuable and adaptable

cultivars, delightful deep rose flowers, 6–7in. in diameter, in abundance all summer. Does well in shallow pools. B.

N. 'Rosita'. Small, purple, stellate flowers, shaded pink. Of little merit. B.

N. 'Rosy Morn'. A delightful American cultivar. Large, stellate shell-pink flowers. B.

N. 'Sanguinea'. Immense crimson-red blooms slightly flecked with white. Stamens orange-red. Olive-green foliage. C, D.

N. 'Seignouretii'. Pretty, rather small, orange-red flowers shading to buff, standing well out of the water. Chestnut-spotted foliage. Very slow to establish. D.

N. 'Sioux'. This is another 'changeable'. The rich chrome-yellow flowers gradually pass through deep orange to coppery red. C.

N. 'Sirius'. Beauty lies in the eye of the beholder they say; this variety has been described as 'delicate fawn lined with red' by one author, and as 'dirty looking fawn' by another. Unless one 'goes' for indeterminate colours, and one has plenty of room, there are so many good colours to choose from it might be as well to stick to them. B.

N. 'Solfatare'. Opens creamy yellow, changes through orange to red. The flowers are stellate, the foliage mottled. C.

N. 'Somptuosa'. Very large globular flowers, rich strawberry-pink, but occupies a small space. Very fragrant. C.

N. 'Souvenir de Jules Jacquier'. A strong grower, large globular mauve-pink flowers, orange stamens, and well worth having. A.

N. 'Speciosa'. Medium sized, flesh-pink. B.

N. 'Splendide'. Dark ruby, medium-sized flowers. B.

N. 'Suavissima'. Very fragrant, rose-pink flowers standing well out of the water. C.

N. 'Sultan'. The flowers are a deep cherry-red shading to darker at the base, flecked white. Green foliage. C.

N. 'Sunrise'. This marvellous American cultivar produces immense, bright yellow fragrant blooms up to 12in. in diameter, the largest flowers amongst hardy water-lilies. The foliage is dark green. Although a strong grower it will adapt to a small pool. B, C.

N. 'Sylphide'. Deep red flowers flaked white, very free flowering. B.

N. tetragona. Widely spread pygmy species originally imported from China, but found in India, Japan, Siberia and Australia also. Having such a wide range there are several geographical forms, varying in minor detail but not cultivated in gardens. The small white flowers are produced freely and they set seed readily. Flowering plants may be raised from seed in one year. D.

N. tuberosa. A North American species which needs plenty of room as the slender creeping rhizomes extend rapidly. Flowers are pure white and sweetly scented, reminiscent of ripe apples. A.

'Poestlingberg'. Probably the most vigorous water-lily we have at our disposal. The foliage bright green, will cover a 10ft. diameter circle the first season; the huge, pure white, solid-textured flowers may attain 12in. across, especially in deep water. May be classed as A for it really should have water 4–5ft. deep over the crown. Naturally, this plant will need plenty of soil, 10cu. ft. of good loam will keep it going for a few years. I have heard of it doing very well in a 10ft. depth of water. It flowers freely.

'Richardsonii'. Globular, pure white flowers, rich green sepals, this is a strong grower for the large pool. Said to be shy flowering but this depends on environment. A.

rosea. Another very strong grower, requiring plenty of room. Medium soft pink flowers, very fragrant. A.

'Rubra'. Deep rosy red flowers with ruby-red stamens, up to 7in. across, but not produced very freely—it produces more foliage than flowers. A, B.

N. 'Tulipiformis'. Huge, deep rose-pink tulip-shaped flowers. B.

N. 'Venusta'. Widely open, rich pink flowers. C.

N. 'Vesuve'. Fair-sized flowers, 5–6in. wide, glowing amaranth-red, of good shape. C.

N. 'Virginia'. Recent American introduction, raised from 'Sun-rise'. Medium large, stellate white flowers, inner petals suffused with gold, bright yellow stamens. Large, light green foliage deepening with age. B.

N. 'Virginalis'. The perfect white water-lily, beautifully shaped, slightly incurved petals, large flowered and fragrant, and flowering all summer. A, B.

N. 'Wm. Doogue'. Large, cup-shaped, delicate pink flowers, ageing to white, very free flowering and vigorous. B.

N. 'William Falconer'. Possibly the darkest ruby-flowered cultivar we have, almost black at the base, while the stamens are bright yellow. Flowers up to 6in. diameter when thoroughly established. The dark red foliage matures to deep green, with red veins. B.

The Tender Water-lilies

No doubt the reason why one so seldom sees plants of tropical water-lilies, in our gardens is the contracting of the average garden space and facilities for growing them. The necessary heating is expensive today, and although there are some cultivars which can be grown in the open pool during the summer months, the preparation of the plants prior to planting them, involving starting them in heat in February or March, and growing them on under glass until the outdoor pool is warm enough to accept them without check, is enough to discourage many would-be growers. Where heated glass is available, and there is the room to spare, nothing could be more attractive than one or two tubs of these fascinating and lovely plants. They can, of course, be enjoyed in the aquatic departments of our botanic gardens, and in certain of the municipal greenhouses up and down the country and at such gardens as Exbury, Chatsworth and many others.

But it is the thrill and joy to be had in growing these beauties oneself that should encourage anyone who has the means and facilities to adventure into these new fields.

The modern dwelling, so often bereft of a garden, may well have a patio or garden room where it may be possible to grow one or more tender water-lilies in tubs or patio pools. Tender water-lilies do not need more than a few inches of water in which to thrive. Incidentally, as it seems to be the custom for the small patio pool to be fitted with a fountain, it should be mentioned that water-lilies and fountains do not mix very well.

By far the greatest number of tender water-lily cultivars is to be found in American lists, for the majority of the hybrid tropicals have been raised in the United States by such experts as Mr George Pring, and by some of the American botanic gardens; new kinds are constantly being raised there, so that there are literally hundreds of named cultivars in that country. It is not possible to describe more than a selection of those most generally grown.

Of the forty or so wild species of tender water-lilies some, such as *N. caerulea*, the so-called Blue Lotus of the Nile, and *N. stellata* from the Far East, are grown in gardens, and others are used by specialists in the production of new hybrids; a few are of little horticultural interest, but will be mentioned in case their names crop up in catalogues. The viviparous tropicals create much interest, for instance the cultivar *N.* 'Daubeyana' (syn. *N. daubeniana*) frequently produces young plants on each leaf, all with young flowers, in addition to the flowers from the main plant. Tropical water-lilies and their hybrids may be separated into two groups: there are those flowering during the day, and the night bloomers. The latter are the strongest growers and may extend into patches up to 15ft. in diameter.

Mostly they have powerful and exquisite perfume, and it is an unforgettable experience visiting a house full of nocturnal blooming nymphaeas.

SPECIES OF TROPICAL WATER-LILY

Nymphaea

N. amazonum. Tropical America, Brazil, Jamaica, Mexico. A nocturnal bloomer; large, yellowish white, floating flowers, bright green, entire foliage, and a perfume of ripe peaches.

N. ampla. Tropical America. Has stellate, white flowers, with golden anthers. Stands well out of water.

N. burtii. Tanganyika. Deep primrose flowers, 8in. across, floating on the surface. Thought to be synonymous with *N. stuhlmannii*, it is a difficult plant to manage, but has been useful in hybridizing—the hybrids are much easier to manage, and propagate readily.

N. caerulea. North and Central Africa. Thought by some to be the Blue Lotus of the Nile, it bears large, sky-blue flowers up to 7in. across, the sepals spotted with black. The flowers remain open from early morning until midnight, they stand well out of the water, and have a delicious perfume.

    albiflora. Rare Egyptian white-flowered variety.

N. calliantha. Tropical Africa. The stellate flowers may be pink, pale blue or purple, with deep yellow stamens.

    tenuis. White or pale blue flowers.

N. capensis. The Cape Blue Water-lily. South Africa, Madagascar. Lovely, very deep sky-blue flowers, sweetly scented, with blue-tipped, yellow stamens. Foliage marbled purple.

forma rubra. Bright rose flowers, sweetly scented, a small grower very suitable for tub cultivation.

madagascariensis. Smaller blue flowers, otherwise typical.

zanzibariensis. Royal Purple Water-lily. Rich purple-blue flowers, yellow stamens tipped navy-blue. Fragrant and free-flowering. It has produced some good hybrids..

N. citrina. East Africa. Possibly a form of *N. stuhlmannii*, it has yellow flowers and is not easily propagated.

N. dentata. Sierra Leone. The large, pure white flowers may exceed 12in. across; the golden stamens are red at the base. Blooms are at their best in the evening. Foliage dentate.

'Grandiflora'. Flowers 15in. diameter and more.

'Magnifica'. Large white flowers, purple spotted stamens.

'Superba' (syn. 'Juno'). Probably the finest white tropical water-lily. Glistening pure white flowers, bright yellow stamens. Probably a true variety, for it comes true from seed.

N. divaricata. N. Rhodesia. The bilobed leaves are submerged, and the pale blue flowers may either be floating or slightly submerged. Will adapt to deep water.

N. elegans. Mexico, Texas. The Senorita Water-lily. Smallish lavender flowers, yellow stamens tipped blue. Very free flowering.

N. flava (syn. *N. mexicana*). Florida, Mexico, Texas. Small, starry yellow flowers, deeper yellow stamens. Ovate green leaves spotted pale brown, purple below. Almost hardy, and may succeed in our warmer counties out of doors.

N. flavo-virens. Mexico. Sweet scented, white, stellate flowers standing well out of the water.

N. gardneriana. Tropical America. Small, reddish flowers. Not often grown.

N. gibertii. Paraguay. Small white flowers without perfume.

N. gigantea. Australia. Immense, sky-blue flowers 12in. across, one of the finest of the day-flowering species. Can be grown success-fully in the outdoor heated pool.

forma media. A much smaller-flowered form.

violacea. Smaller, darker blue flowers.

N. gracilis. Mexico. Large white, perfumed like lily-of-the-valley, this species has been used widely for hybridization. It is thought to be a form either of *N. flavo-virens*, or possibly synonymous with it.

'Azurea'. Similar, but the flowers are pale blue.

'Purpurea'. Rich purple flowers.

'Rosea'. Pink flowers.

'Rubra'. Red flowers. All fine introduced forms.

N. heudelottii. Central Africa. A pygmy tropical, tiny pale blue flowers. *Nana* is the smallest tropical variety.

N. jamesoniana. Ecuador. Small brownish yellow flowers.

N. lotus. Egypt and Africa. The White Lotus of the Nile. This night-blooming species has large flowers, deliciously scented, white, tinted pink.

   pubescens. Australia, Java, Philippines, India. Smaller, white flowers, green stamens. Sweetly scented.

N. micrantha (syn. *N. vivipara*). West Africa. Similar to *N. caerulea*, but has the viviparous habit. Bluish white flowers, this species can be grown in quite a small container.

N. ovalifolia. East Africa. Small blue flowers.

N. polychroma. Tanganyika. Large, bright blue flowers with deep violet stamens. Instead of the more usual upright tuber, the rhizome is horizontal, and propagates readily by budding along the rhizome. Does well indoors in England.

N. primulina. Rhodesia. Good-sized primrose-yellow flowers well above the water, purplish foliage.

N. rubra. India, Brazil. Nocturnal bloomer. Bright red flowers, cinnabar stamens, bronzy crimson foliage ageing green. The flowers may be 6–10in. across. Not often grown but the parent of some fine hybrids.

N. rudgeana. South America, Jamaica. Nocturnal. Small, lemon-scented, greenish white flowers.

N. stellata. South-east Asia, Java, Philippines, Africa. Has stellate, light blue flowers, and will do well in the outdoor heated pool. It is similar but inferior to N. *caerulea*.

   rosea. A fine plant. Soft rose flowers larger than the type. Day flowering.

N. stemaspidota. Brazil. A small-growing plant with large, deep crimson flowers.

N. stuhlmannii. Africa. Large, bright yellow flowers, orange stamens, very sweetly scented, has been used widely for crossing with other species.

N. zenkeri. Cameroons. White flowers 2–3in. wide.

DAY-FLOWERING HYBRIDS AND CULTIVARS

Nymphaea

N. 'A. Siebert'. Free-flowering, bright rose.

N. 'African Gold'. A new fine clear yellow.

N. 'Albert-le-Lestang'. This is a *gigantea* hybrid, whose large white flowers are tinted blue, and the stamens have a purplish base.

N. 'American Beauty'. Large reddish flowers, lemon-yellow centre, handsome foliage.

N. 'Amethyst'. Viviparous. The flowers are a true amethyst-blue.

N. 'Antoinette Chaize'. Lavender-blue, tipped gentian-blue.

N. 'August Koch'. Viviparous. A fine oldish cultivar flowering freely throughout summer and winter in a warm house. The 7–8in. flowers are a rich violet-blue, with reddish stamens, and cut well. Excellent for tub cultivation.

N. 'Aviator Pring'. New, large-flowered primrose-yellow, which propagates well and is sometimes viviparous.

N. 'Baghdad'. Viviparous. Pale purplish blue, just above the water.

N. 'B. C. Berry'. A striking ruby-crimson.

N. 'Blue Beauty' (syn. *N. pulcherrima*, *N.* 'Pennsylvania' (*caerulea* × *zanzibariensis*). Immense, deep blue flowers often 12in. across, golden stamens with violet anthers. Dark green leaves with tapering lobes.

N. 'Blue Bird'. Very fine viviparous cultivar with deep blue flowers.

N. 'Blue Triumph'. Blue flowers often 12in. across, in profusion, the green foliage is flecked bronze.

N. 'Bob Trickett'. Huge campanula-blue flowers, 12–14in. across, cup-shaped.

N. 'Castalliflora'. Raised from interbreeding forms of *N. capensis zanzibariensis rosea*. Large, pale pink flowers, bright pink anthers on yellow stamens. Handsome, serrated mottled foliage.

N. 'Celeste'. Viviparous. Violet flowers.

N. 'Chicago'. Clear pink flowers.

N. 'Cleveland'. Fragrant, clear rose-pink flowers, mottled leaves.

N. 'Colonel Lindbergh'. One of the finest. Broad-petalled, large, deep sky-blue flowers on long stems. Very fragrant.

N. 'Daisy'. Viviparous. A recent, large, white-flowered form.

N. 'Daubeyana'. One of the most popular viviparous cultivars, very good in shallow water. Practically every leaf produces plantlets which flower in addition to the main flowers, which are small and light blue. Ideal for tub cultivation.

N. 'Director G. T. Moore'. Unique, true navy-blue flowers, 8–10in. across. Small, rich purple leaves.

N. 'Eastonensis'. Steely blue flowers, deeply serrated foliage.

N. 'Edward C. Elliott'. Lovely pale pink flowers, yellow, pink-tipped stamens, flowers often 10in. wide.

N. 'Emily Grant Hutchings'. Bell-shaped, amaranth-shaded flowers.

N. 'Francois Treyve'. Free flowering, indigo-blue.

N. 'General Pershing' ('Mrs Whitaker' × 'Castalliflora'). Considered by many the most beautiful of the tropical water-lilies. The large, chalice-shaped blooms are a warm pink, very fragrant, the yellow stamens are tipped rose.

N. 'Golden West'. Salmon-pink, ageing to apricot, and golden stamens. The foliage is mottled red.

N. 'Henkeliana'. Unusual, flat blue flowers, sweet violet scent.

N. 'Henry Shaw'. An old favourite, open saucer-shaped, fragrant flowers, light bluebell-blue; chrome-yellow stamens. Flowers all day and is adapted to small pools.

N. 'Independence'. A rich pink-flowered, viviparous cultivar—unusual, since viviparous cultivars are mostly blue.

N. 'Independence Blue'. Exactly the same as the foregoing, except that the flowers are blue.

N. 'Isabella Pring'. Viviparous. Immense pure white, very double, crispy and very fragrant, one of the first white hybrids.

N. 'Janice'. The first viviparous white. Attractive bell-shaped flowers.

N. 'Judge Hitchcock'. Medium flowers up to 8in. cup-like, violet, paler in the centre, the golden stamens are tipped blue.

N. 'Jupiter'. Large, fine-textured, deep purple. Intensely fragrant.

N. 'King of the Blues'. Free-flowering, deep navy-blue flowers.

N. 'Listeri'. Medium-sized, rich blue.

N. 'L. Dittmann'. Very vigorous, rose-coloured flowers.

N. 'Madame Abel Chatenay'. Lavender-blue flowers, mottled foliage.

N. 'Madame Herbert Cutbush'. Attractive, long-tapering, ageratum-blue flowers.

N. 'Margaret Mary'. New. Miniature tropical, viviparous, small enough to grow in a sunny window. Baby blue stellate flowers 2in. across.

N. 'Maynardii'. Huge, pale heliotrope flowers.

N. 'Micheliana'. Rosy lilac flowers.

N. 'Midnight'. Very floriferous, flowers small, deep purple, small golden centre.

N. 'Mrs C. W. Ward'. Large flowered, over 10 in. diameter, rich rose-pink, with a large boss of golden stamens, the flowers stand well out of the water.

N. 'Mrs George H. Pring'. A pure white raised from Mrs Whitaker, otherwise very similar.

N. 'Mrs Whitaker'. Huge 12in. blooms of pale lavender, ageing to milk-white. The pale yellow stamens are tipped lavender. Does well in a tub.

N. 'Mrs Woodrow Wilson'. Viviparous. Enormous lavender-blue flowers, of firm texture. The form 'Gigantea' is even larger.

N. 'Pamela'. Large, saucer-shaped, deep sky-blue flowers, broad petals, standing up well. Marbled foliage.

N. 'Panama Pacific'. Viviparous. Medium flowers, deep vinous blue darkening to deep royal purple. Will flower all the year round if kept warm enough. Easily grown.

N. 'Patricia'. Viviparous. Small grower, masses of crimson flowers.

N. 'Peach Blow'. Large, very double, rounded flowers, lovely pale rose, many golden stamens, handsome foliage. Viviparous.

N. 'Pink Delight'. Carmine-pink.

N. 'Pink Pearl'. Medium silvery pink, pink-tipped stamens, a continuous bloomer.

N. 'Pink Platter'. Viviparous. Long petals, wide open pink flowers, pink-tipped stamens. Brown-flecked foliage.

N. 'Reine d'Italie'. Tyrolean purple, strawberry-red stamens.

N. 'Rio Rita'. Wide open flowers, deep pink, almost red, broad petals. Small foliage flecked mahogany.

N. 'Royal Purple'. Viviparous. Glowing purple flowers, 6–8in. wide.

N. 'St. Louis'. One of the first yellow tropicals, stellate, 10-in. flowers. Deeper yellow centre. Mottled foliage.

N. 'St Louis Gold'. Medium sized, citron-yellow. Large, dark green leaves, flushed chocolate.

N. 'Shell Pink'. Resembles 'General Pershing', but is a clearer shade of pink. Handsome spotted foliage. Weakly viviparous.

Star lilies. A group of well tried older cultivars, stellate flowers standing well above the water. Amongst the hardiest of the tropicals, and very prolific.

'Pink Star'. Pale pink and lavender.

'Red Star'. Clear red, not so free as the others.

'White Star'. Waxy white.

'Yellow Star'. Large, yellow, rather flat flowers.

N. 'Stella Gurney'. Large, stellate, evenly-toned pink flowers.

N. 'Sunbeam'. New. Regarded as the most brilliant yellow, large flowered. Viviparous.

N. 'Talisman'. Viviparous. Fine red and yellow flowers.

N. 'Wild Rose'. Viviparous. Large petals, bright pink, large golden centre. Foliage dark green, flecked mahogany.

N. 'William Stone'. Outstanding. Large amaranth-shaded, violet-blue flowers remaining open all day long.

N. 'William Ward'. A *zanzibariensis* hybrid, large rose flowers.

NIGHT-FLOWERING HYBRIDS AND CULTIVARS

Nymphaea

N. 'Adele'. Carmine-magenta flowers.

N. 'Albert d'Argence'. Magenta-red flowers, orange-red stamens.

N. 'Armand Millet'. Bright purple-red flowers, large size, foliage green, deeply toothed.

N. 'Arnoldiana'. Medium flowers, rosy carmine.

N. 'Bissetii'. Large, 8–10in. flowers of delicate pale pink, with broad petals; the dentate green leaves are shot with bronze.

N. 'Boucheana'. This also has very broad petals, of rosy pink.

N. 'Columbiana'. Very dark red flowers, a fine contrast to the paler hybrids, and dark bronze leaves.

N. 'Deaniana'. An old cultivar with clear pink, cup-shaped blooms.

N. 'Delicatissima'. The dark metallic foliage contrasts well with the pale pink flowers.

N. 'Devonshire'. Another old cultivar, but one of the best. Immense bright red flowers, which light up well at night. A very strong grower needing plenty of room.

N. 'Diana'. Medium flowers, carmine-rose.

'Grandiflora'. Larger blooms, darker in hue.

N. 'Dr Florenze'. Dark red flowers, fine by artificial light.

N. 'Frank Trelease'. Huge deep crimson flowers, deep mahogany stamens, and leaves dark bronzy red. The flowers glow when artificially lit.

N. 'George Huster'. Perhaps the finest of the tropical kinds, the deep velvety crimson flowers have a special richness at night. The foliage is reddish bronze.

N. 'H. C. Haarstick'. The large flowers have long petals of brilliant red, red-gold stamens. Needs plenty of space.

N. 'Indica Brahma'. Fiery rose flowers.

'Hofgartendirektor Graebner'. Deeper rose flowers, deepening towards the centre. Dentate, reddish brown foliage.

'Isis'. Delicate pink, wide concave petals.

'Spira'. Similar but a darker hue.

N. 'James Gurney Junior'. The crimson flowers age to deep purple-red.

N. 'Jubilee'. Large white flowers, tinted pink, up to 8in. across, deeply-toothed foliage.

N. 'Jules Vachero'. Vivid red flowers. Very free flowering.

N. 'Juno'. See under *N. dentata* 'Superba', p. 91.

N. 'Kewensis'. An old cultivar raised at Kew and still grown, it has delicate pink flowers, mottled green foliage.

N. 'Krumbiegelii'. Carmine-red flowers.

N. 'Laelia'. Flowers of delicate orchid-pink.

'Colorans'. Darker coloured flowers.

N. 'La Reine de los Angeles'. The large 10-in. flowers are broad petalled, and of a glistening pure white.

N. 'Madame Auguste Tezier'. This unique cultivar has violet-heliotrope flowers deepening to the centre, and brownish stamens. The purple foliage is deeply dentate.

N. 'Marie Lagrange'. The rose-purple petals have a median stripe of white, stamens yellow.

N. 'Mars'. Bright rosy vermilion.

N. 'Minerva'. Large, white, cup-shaped blooms.

N. 'Missouri'. The huge 14-in. blooms are very double, and a glistening white which gleam in the evening light. The flowers last several days, and the plant needs plenty of room to spread the maroon-splashed green foliage.

N. 'Mrs George C. Hitchcock'. Huge, rose-pink flowers, mahogany stamens. Stands well out of the water.

N. 'O'Marana'. The glowing red flowers attain 12in. in diameter, and each petal has a central thin white line. As the flowers age, the deep orange stamens become prominent. Bronzy red deeply-toothed foliage.
N. 'Ortgiesiana'. Large, creamy white flowers with purple base. 'Rubra'. This old cultivar is still grown. Very free flowering, clear pink.
N. 'President Girard'. Medium-sized, rosy carmine flowers.
N. 'Pride of California'. Beautifully-shaped, blood-red flowers, held well above the water. Free flowering.
N. 'Rufus J. Lackland'. Crimson ageing to deep purple.
N. 'Smithiana'. Creamy white flowers with yellow stamens.
N. 'Sturtevantii'. Strong grower needing much space to produce its bronze-crimson foliage. Huge rosy pink flowers, cup-shaped. Orange-brown stamens.

Victoria regia (*V. amazonica*; the second of these names is the more correct, but the plant is widely known by the older name, and it has therefore been given priority). One can hardly leave the tropical water-lilies without some mention of this amazing plant, though it is unlikely that the amateur of today will go to the trouble and expense of growing such a giant, when they can be seen in our botanic gardens. A temperature of 85 °F. (30 °C.) and a pool at least 20ft. wide, with a great deal of rich loam, is needed to accommodate one plant. It is grown from seed each year, as a rule; though it is a perennial it is better to treat it as an annual. The seeds are sown at about the end of January, in pans of sterilized loam, immersed in water, in full light. In nature *V. regia* grows in deep water, 6ft. or more, but in cultivation it is usual to grow it in about 2ft. at most, a depth easier to keep up to the warmth required.

The enormous leaves in nature may attain a breadth of 7–8ft., with upturned edges 2–8in. deep, and will bear the weight of a child quite safely. The total area covered by one plant may exceed 600sq. ft. The equally enormous flowers, often over 1ft. across, are nocturnal, open white, gradually ageing to purplish red, and disseminate a perfume of ripe pineapples. The fruit, as large as a baby's head, is protected by strong spines, and contains many large shiny seeds. These are used by the Indians for food.

Many attempts to establish this plant during the reign of Queen Victoria, after whom the plant was named, failed until 1849, when it was flowered at Chatsworth, from whence seed was distributed. Other species are *V. cruziana*, successfully established in North America towards the end of the last century, and *V. randii*, also raised in North America.

Victoria cruziana will grow at a slightly lower temperature, 75 °F. (24 °C.), flowers earlier than *V. regia*, and has foliage of a lighter green. The victorias all come from South America, *V. regia* from Bolivia, *V. randii* from Brazil, and *V. cruziana* from Paraguay.

Another member of the *Nymphaeaceae*, the Indian gorgon plant, *Euryale ferox*, was regarded as the monster of the water-lily world until the victorias were discovered. This plant has leaves 2–3ft. across, but without the turned-up edges, and the flowers are small and bluish violet. The seeds are used for food in India and China. The whole plant is clothed with vicious spines. It is treated as an annual, and sows itself in outdoor pools in North America as far north as Philadelphia, but needs warm greenhouse treatment in this country. It is seldom grown except in botanic gardens.

The Nelumbos and Nuphars

Nelumbo (the lotus) is one of the most ancient plants we have in cultivation, its history goes back to the Cretaceous period, some 130,000,000 years ago, when it grew much farther north than it does today, for fossil remains of nelumbo have been found in many European deposits of that age. Since recorded human history, this plant has been the object of veneration, right up to the present day, as well as being valued for its economic uses. The lotus has been cited as a parallel to the emergence of goodness from evil in human affairs, the glorious foliage and flowers thrusting up from the corruption and filth which nourishes the roots. Buddha is said to be seated on a lotus, which no doubt contributes to his benign expression.

From the gardener's point of view the nelumbos are a family of great interest and beauty, well worth a good deal of trouble. The great peltate leaves are waterproofed by a secretion of wax, so that raindrops run about the surface like quicksilver, a source of fascination to young and old, while the flowers, like huge peonies, have great beauty and wonderful fragrance.

Unfortunately, these plants cannot be grown outdoors in England, all the year round, though they can be grown in the open during the summer months without artificial heat. However, their rhizomes do not ripen sufficiently under these circumstances to survive the winter under cover. Nelumbo grows very well in the open in parts of Italy, and southern Europe. In Vienna they survive quite well if covered with a foot or so of dry leaves during the winter. In Britain, however, they are best grown under glass the whole year round, for their rhizomes develop and ripen so much better under glass. They should be grown in the sunniest part of the greenhouse to encourage thorough ripening of the growths.

Nelumbo

N. lutea (syn. *Nelumbium luteum*). American Lotus, Duck Acorn. This is the North American Lotus, and is found from south Ontario southwards in stagnant pools. It is hardy where there is enough sun heat to ripen the root stocks and where the frost does not penetrate down to them. The leaves are up to 2ft. wide and stand more than 2ft. out of the water. Unfortunately, this species does not flower until it has been established several years, but when it does the flowers are sulphur-yellow and up to 10in. across.

flavescens. This variety has smaller flowers but produces them in greater abundance.

N. nucifera (syn. *Nelumbium nuciferum*, *N. indicum*). Hindu Lotus. India, Philippines, Japan, north Australia. This beautiful species bears truly magnificent flowers a foot across, a brilliant rose in colour, paling as the flower ages. The foliage has a silvery sheen and stands well above the water.

alba (Magnolia Lotus). A white-flowered form.

grandiflora. Huge, single, white fragrant flowers.

'Striata'. Pure white flowers, the petals are edged red.

'Virens'. Double, pure white flowers, striped sea-green. The stripes disappear as the flower ages to pure white.

'Gigantea'. Very large flowers, rich rosy purple with a delicate fragrance. Huge, deep green leaves.

'Shiroman' (syn. *alba plena*). Japan. Immense, double cream flowers which fade to pure white as the flowers age. Very floriferous and fragrant.

These are the two most well-known species; other desirable plants are:

N. 'Grössherzog Ernst Ludwig' (*lutea* 'Flavescens' × 'Osiris'). Huge, globular, rich rose flowers with a powerful fragrance, bright yellow stamens. The foliage is a powdery blue-green.

N. japonica 'Rubra'. Huge, double flowers over 1ft. across, white, overlaid rose. Blue-green foliage.

N. 'Kermesiana'. A prolific Japanese cultivar, white flowers washed with rose.

N. 'Osiris'. Deep rose, cup-shaped flowers, a strong grower.

N. 'Pekinensis Rubra' (syn. 'Peking'). Large, rosy carmine flowers, very fragrant, and splendid foliage.

    'Plena' (syn. 'Red Peking'). Double-flowered cultivar; this and the previous one are amongst the darkest coloured forms.

N. 'Pulchra'. Huge, 1ft. wide flowers, deep rosy lilac, lined and edged red. A strong grower. Floriferous.

N. pygmaea 'Alba'. A miniature, growing about 1½ft., with single white flowers 5–6in. across.

    'Plena'. Double dwarf white.

    'Rosea' (syn. 'Dawn'). Small, bright rose flowers.

    'Plena' (syn. 'Double Dawn'). Very double rosy pink, free flowering and strong.

N. 'Violacea'. Deep purplish red, streaked white. Not free flowering.

There is a new strain of nelumbo being developed in America which is said to be easily grown in quite small containers, ideal for patio decoration. We shall look forward to seeing them in Britain.

THE NUPHARS (NENUPHAR)

Where the true nymphaeas will not thrive and where some similar foliage is required, there is a place in the water garden for the nuphars. This is a genus of very hardy and rather rampageous water plants which will thrive in warm or cold water, still or running, and in any depth from 6ft. to 6in. In the deeper waters some varieties have beautiful submerged leaves, thin textured, translucent, and waved, and on this account are decorative plants for the very large aquarium.

    The leaves resemble those of the water-lilies; in deep water they float on the surface, in shallow water they usually stand well out and provide a certain variety of marginal foliage for the larger pools and lakes. The flowers are of no great account, for the conspicuous part is confined to the sepals, the petals being reduced to stamen-like objects. Planting and cultivation is exactly the same as for the hardy water-lilies; the thick rhizomes are firmly planted in loam with the growing point projecting out of the soil. It may be advisable to anchor the roots by placing a stone on top of the rhizome, as this is so buoyant that it may come loose and be found floating on the surface the next day. Of course, as soon as new roots are formed they will hold the plant firmly. The nuphars grow very well in slight shade, but they flower much more freely in the open sunshine. Very few species are grown by commercial growers. The following species and varieties may be offered from time to time.

Nuphar

N. advena. Common Spatterdock, Cow Lily. North America. One of the better species, adapted to still or running water. The large, thick, bright green leaves are oblong-ovate, with a deep, widely-open sinus, and are about a foot long. The flowers are 2–3in. across, globular, yellow tinged green or dull purple. There is a variegated form found in British Columbia, with purplish yellow flowers. The leaves usually float and do not stand out of the water as in the type, and the basal sinus is closed.

N. japonica. Longish sagittate leaves on the surface, and crispy submerged leaves. Flowers yellow, 2–3in. across.

  rubrotincta. Orange-scarlet sepals, and red-tipped stamens. The dark olive-green leaves stand out of the water. There is a giant form with larger leaves and flowers, but their colour is less vivid.

  variegata. Erect foliage, mottled with creamy white. Yellow flowers. All the Japanese species require still water.

N. lutea. Brandy-bottle. Britain, Europe. Received its popular name on account of the flask-shaped fruit. The flowers have a distinctly alcoholic odour—in Greece a drink is prepared from the flowers, whether to capture the odour or not is not known. This species grows commonly in moving water in Britain, often in deep lakes, when it produces fine, transparent, submerged foliage. The bright green, floating leaves are 8–10in. long, the flowers yellow. There are several geographical forms and varieties.

N. macrophylla. This strong-growing species from the southern states of North America has large, bright green, oblong-ovate leaves, but the flowers are not more than an inch across.

N. microphylla (syn. *N. kalmiana*). North America. This is a much smaller species, leaves 3–4in. wide and yellow flowers 1in. wide. Planted near the pool edge it spreads rapidly, and flowers very freely. The submerged foliage is very decorative in the aquarium.

N. orbiculata. Southern states of America. Bright green, circular leaves with crisped margins, flowers 2in. across, yellowish. The stems and undersurface of leaves are downy.

N. polysepala. North America. One of the largest species, the yellow flowers are 4–5in. across, the leaves are elongated, and stand up well in shallow water. In deeper water they float on the surface.

N. pumila (syn. *N. minima*). Dwarf Pond Lily. Britain, Europe. Quite a worthwhile plant for planting the edges of rock garden streams and pools where it grows readily and flowers freely. The yellow flowers are about 1in. across, the foliage is tiny.

N. rubrodisca. North America. Red-disked Pond Lily. Elongated leaves, 3–10in. long, standing up out of the water when this is shallow, floating in deeper water. The 1½in. flowers are yellow, with a prominent reddish crimson centre.

Marginal Planting

To complete the garden picture around the pool, contrasts are needed to balance the predominantly horizontal lines of water and water-lilies. And to present a natural appearance to the informal pool, these plants should grow in the water near to the pool margin, as well as being merged into plantings in the surrounding ground. The vertical lines of various reeds and rushes, iris, typha and acorus, and the very varied outlines and textures of many other aquatics, all blend to complete a satisfying composition, always provided that the plants are arranged with care so that each makes its own contribution to the whole. The following list of 'marginal' aquatics is by no means exhaustive, for there are many hundreds of species in this category which are more of interest to the taxonomist than the gardener. Those plants requiring winter protection are mentioned after the reliably hardy ones have been dealt with.

I have mentioned in an earlier chapter a method of dealing with rapidly spreading water plants, that is, to confine the creeping rhizomes in solid-sided and bottomed containers, lowered into the water to the correct depth and to replant whenever the rhizomes start to wander away from the containers.

Acorus (Araceae)
A genus of hardy herbaceous plants well-known for their aromatic and medicinal properties. They should be planted in shallow water or moist soil adjacent to water. Propagation is by division of rhizomes in spring.
A. calamus. Sweet Flag, Beewort. An iris-like plant with long linear foliage, prominent parallel veins; the flowering stems leaf-like with a thick midrib, from which, near the tip, projects the

2–3in. spadix, densely covered with greenish flowers. This spadix is inconspicuous. When crushed, the roots emit a pleasant scent. About 2ft. high, this plant is rather too invasive for the small garden, and is best planted at the edges of large pools and lakes. It grows wild in Britain, having been introduced in the seventeenth century.

'Variegatus'. A much more valuable plant, this has foliage conspicuously variegated with creamy white, and is well worthwhile for the medium pool if planted in a solid-walled container.

A. gramineus. Japan. A much more dwarf species, 8–12in., making compact tuffets. Very shallow water or moist margin.

'Pusillus'. Japan. Very dwarf, 3–4in. Narrow, sword-shaped leaves in dense tufts, a good carpeter in moist soil near the pool's edge.

'Variegatus'. The leaves are striped with pale creamy yellow.

Alisma (Alismataceae). Water Plantain

A group of rather charming aquatics, with graceful panicles of many tiny, pale lilac flowers. The flowerheads should be removed before seed is set, or seedlings will appear all over the place. The roots contain acrid principles of medicinal use.

A. lanceolatum. Widely distributed, Britain, Europe, India, S. America. Narrow, oblong-lanceolate leaves with acute tip, pinkish white flowers. 1–1½ft. Shallow water.

A. plantago-aquatica. Great Water Plaintain. A really charming plant for shallow water. Long stalked elliptic leaves, pyramidal panicles of tiny rose-coloured flowers in profusion, perennial. 2–3ft. Prevent seeding.

A. ranunculoides (more correctly, but less well-known as *Echinodorus ranunculodes*). Britain, N. Africa. Lanceolate foliage, rosy flowers. 12in.

A. subcordata (syn. *A. parviflorum*). American Water Plantain. North America. Rare species, one of the prettiest. Rounded foliage, panicles of rosy flowers. 1½ft. Shallow water, 3–5in. deep, is preferred.

Aponogeton (Aponogetonaceae)

A group of valuable aquatics, most of which are tender. There are, however, two species of great garden merit. They form tubers from which slender stalks rise to the surface, where the expanded leaf blade floats on the surface. Easily propagated from seed.

A. distachyus. Water Hawthorn, Cape Pond-Weed. Africa, Australia. One of the most attractive water plants, perfectly hardy. Strap-shaped leaves, green or purplish brown, float on the surface, and the forked inflorescence rises 2 in. above the water. It bears closely packed, pure white flowers with jet-black anthers, and emits a powerful hawthorn fragrance, especially towards evening. It seeds itself readily. The tubers should be planted in loam 1–1½ft. below the surface. A word of warning. If your pool has a high population of the water-snail *Limnaea stagnalis*, do not plant any aponogetons until you have eliminated the snails; they will dispose of newly planted *A. distachyus* overnight.

'Aldenhamensis' is a greatly improved form with larger flowers, and stouter growths; the leaves have a bronzed purplish suffusion. There are other forms which have been described, such as *A. d.* 'Roseus', but it is doubtful if they are obtainable today.

A. krauseanus. Africa, Australia. This species is a most beautiful plant, requiring a sheltered sunny pool in the warmer parts of the country. The sweetly scented flowers are much daintier than those of *A. distachyus*; they stand several inches out of the water and are of a warm tone of creamy sulphur. The plant sets seed feely, and it would be a wise precaution in colder districts to save seed and sow it in sterilized loam under water in a cool greenhouse, or if tender water-lilies are grown all the year round, a few standby plants might well be grown with the lilies.

Butomus (Butomaceae). Flowering Rush

B. umbellatus. Native, Europe, temperate Asia. A valuable plant for its umbels of pink flowers at midsummer. The flower heads resemble those of agapanthus, on a smaller scale. The triquetrous deep green leaves are bronze when young, sword-shaped, sometimes twisted. It grows to 2–2½ft. The rhizomes creep, branch freely and afford a ready means of increase by dividing them in spring. Plant in 2–3in. of water.

Calla (Araceae). Bog Arum

C. palustris. Europe, North America, North Asia. An invaluable plant for the pool margin, the creeping stems bear glossy cordate leaves, the flowers are little white 'arums' in summer, followed by spikes of scarlet fruits in autumn—like those of a miniature wake-robin. It seldom exceeds 9in. and thrives in shallow water of 2–3in., and even in wet soil adjoining the pool. The attractive foliage contrasts well with other aquatics.

Caltha (Ranunculaceae). Marsh Marigold, Kingcup, Water Cowslip

The first bog plants to flower, often in March, the marsh marigolds are indispensable for the waterside. In caltha, the flowers are composed of sepals—the true petals are missing.

C. leptosepala. North America. A rather rare species with narrow silvery sepals, but the dark green foliage resembles that of our native *C. palustris.*

'Grandiflora'. A form with larger flowers.

C. natans. Arctic America, North Asia. Slender creeping stems, orbicular foliage, white to pink flowers.

C. palustris. Water Blobs, Kingcup, Marsh Marigold. North temperate zone. Our native marsh marigold is one of the most showy of bog plants, prodigal in its display of large golden flowers in March. It grows 9–12in. high.

'Alba'. This Himalayan variety differs in having white sepals.

'Flore-pleno'. The most conspicuous object in the spring water garden, with very double flowers.

'Plena'. Large-flowered, very double, and flowering a little later than the preceding. The stamens have all been converted into sepals and it is sometimes known as *monstrosa plena.*

C. plurisepala. Conspicuous, rich yellow, semi-double flowers. 12in. in height.

C. polypetala. Giant Marsh Marigold. East Europe, Asia Minor. A very showy species, from 2–3ft. tall with large yellow flowers, 2½in. wide, in profusion. Spreading rapidly, this is a plant for the larger pool; the flower stems become decumbent when the flowers are dead and root at the nodes, forming additional plants. Plant in very shallow water, or in the bog.

Cotula (Compositae)

C. coronopifolia. Golden Buttons. South Africa, but naturalized in many countries, including Britain. Annual, sometimes perennial, this plant seeds freely and establishes itself in shallow water. Aromatic foliage, small rayless golden flowers in great profusion. 6in.

Decodon (syn. Nesaea) (Lythraceae). Swamp Loose-strife, Water-Willow

D. verticillatus. North America. Shrubby perennial with wand-like branches 5–10ft. long, lanceolate foliage and whorls of purple flowers in the leaf axils. The shoots bend over and root at the tips in the mud. Brilliant crimson autumn colour. A fine plant for naturalizing in boggy areas.

Houttuynia (Saururaceae)

H. cordata. Himalaya, China, Japan. Rather a charming plant, metallic, blue-green cordate leaves, red stems, and a terminal, cone-shaped inflorescence of small white flowers, with four basal snow-white bracts. It grows 2ft. tall. Requires a deep strong loam in 2–3in. water. There is a rare double variety.

Hydrocleys (Alismaceae)

H. commersonii (syn. *H. humboldtii, Limnocharis humboldtii, L. commersonii, L. nymphaeoides, Stratiotes nymphaeoides, Vespuccia humboldtii*). Water Poppy. A very beautiful aquatic, not reliably hardy except perhaps in the warmest counties, but well worth growing even if pieces must be wintered in a greenhouse. The thick, oval, floating leaves are accompanied by large 2½-in. three-petalled, light yellow flowers. The individual flowers last but a day, but a succession of new flowers appear all summer. It requires a 9-in. depth of water.

Hypericum (Guttiferae). St John's Wort

H. elodes. Marsh St. John's Wort. Europe, including Britain.
Attractive, opposite small leaves covered with silvery hairs, borne
on reddish prostrate stems. Soft yellow flowers in summer.
Requires an acid soil and grows well in very shallow water.

Iris (Iridaceae)

There are a great many iris species which are admirable for waterside planting, but not actually in the water. A selection of the
latter kinds will be dealt with in a later chapter (p. 139). The only
iris which will grow in water or in waterlogged soil without
deterioration are the beardless iris, *I. laevigata*, *I. pseudacorus* and *I.
versicolor*.

I. kaempferi. This is a borderline case, as this species likes to be wet
all summer, but is better raised above water level in winter. On
the other hand, for the last twenty years I have had growing in
water continuously a fine cultivar under the name *I. k.* 'Purple
East' and it is thriving. It has all the botanical characters attributed
to *I. kaempferi*.

I. laevigata. This fine species has been regarded by many writers as
synonymous with *I. kaempferi*, but there are distinct and easily
recognizable differences between the two. When hybrids are
being considered, it may be difficult to decide to which species
they should be assigned. Briefly, the visible differences are as follows.
The leaves in *I. kaempferi* have a strongly marked midrib, whereas
those of *I. laevigata* have not. In *I. kaempferi* the standards are much
shorter than the falls, but in *I. laevigata* they are almost as long as
the falls. The seed capsules of *I. kaempferi* are short and broad, on
long pedicels, but those of *I. laevigata* are oblong, on short pedicels.
The seeds of *I. kaempferi* are thin and circular, those of *I. laevigata*
thick and semicircular. *I. laevigata* is a true bog plant and thrives
in 3–4in. of water in deep loamy soil. The flowers are a rich blue
with a golden spot or streak and they appear in June. *I. laevigata*
comes from Japan and East Asia. This species has been grown for
many years by Japanese specialists, and several doubles have been
raised, though to Western eyes this is a doubtful advantage.

'Alba'. A pure white cultivar, a fine contrast with the type.

'Atropurpurea'. Rich violet flowers.

'Benikiren'. A recent Japanese novelty, the blue flowers are
mottled with silver.

'Colchesteri'. An old cultivar but very good, the large flowers
are pure white, mottled rich blue. A.M., R.H.S.

'Elegantissima' (syn. 'Variegata). A very beautiful plant, the
foliage is green and white and the flowers an attractive soft blue.
2ft. in height.

'Niagara'. New. Large bluish white flowers.

'Perfield Beauty'. New. Very large purple-blue flowers, each
fall veined white.

'Regal'. One of the loveliest, the large flowers are a rich royal
purple, freely produced, 2½ft. in height. A.M., R.H.S.

'Rose Queen'. The flowers of this cultivar are smaller than the
type, but are of a delightful soft rose colour. 2ft. in height.
A.M., R.H.S. Has *I. kaempferi*-type foliage.

'Snowdrift'. The largest-flowering cultivar, six petals of pure
white, yellow at the base, 2½ft. in height.

'Zambesi'. A lovely sky-blue, falls long and pendent.

I. pseudacorus. Yellow Water Iris. Europe, North Africa, Asia
Minor, Siberia. This very ancient plant has been found as a fossil,
and today grows very commonly in Britain, in marshes and along
streamsides. The flowers, on 3-ft. stems, have almost circular
blades for the falls, often with a central veining of brown-purple.
The standards vary in shape and size from an inch with a small
blade, to mere tubercles. The stout rhizome is very tough, and is
pink when cut open. This is the original 'fleur-de-lis'.

'Bastardii'. This form has soft primrose flowers, very free
flowering, but not so vigorous as the type plant. A rather rare
form, it occurs occasionally in batches of seedlings of *I. pseudacorus* itself.

'Golden Queen'. Large-flowered, deep golden-yellow cultivar,
slightly taller than the type.

'Variegatus'. One of the most conspicuous waterside plants in
early summer, the foliage is creamy yellow, darkening slightly
as the year ages. Bright yellow flowers. Seedlings seem to be
unable to pass on the variegation, but all forms may be propagated readily by division in spring, or after flowering. Seed
affords a ready means of raising the type in quantity.

I. versicolor. For all practical purposes a purple flowered *I. pseuda-*

corus, except that the standards are rather more than half the length of the falls, and are lanceolate. The purple blade of the falls is veined purple on orange at the base, fading to white. The flowers vary from slaty-purple and blue, to purple.

'Kermesina'. A deep red-flowered cultivar. 2½ft.

In nature *I. versicolor* varies a good deal from one district to another, both in colour and stature, and it might be worthwhile raising from seed collected from good forms when one comes across them. *I. virginica* is probably such a form.

Limnanthemum (Gentianaceae)

L. peltatum (syn. *L. nymphoides*, *Nymphoides peltata*, *Villarsia nymphaeoides*). Water Fringe. Europe, including Britain, North America. Rather rampant, but a useful plant. The cordate mottled leaves, 2in. across, resemble those of a miniature water-lily, and arise from creeping stems which root and form new crowns at each node. In summer a succession of fringed golden-yellow flowers appear, standing 2–3in. above the water. Should be confined in a solid-walled container.

'Bennettii'. A form with clear green leaves without mottling, otherwise similar. 2–6in. of water is required.

Lobelia (Lobeliaceae)

A large genus which contains four suitable water plants.

L. cardinalis. Cardinal Flower. North America. Rosettes of green, sometimes purple, lanceolate foliage, 2–2½ft. spikes of pure scarlet lobelia flowers of good size. Thrives in shallow water.

L. dortmanni. Water Lobelia. Western Europe, Britain. Found in acid waters in Wales, the Lakes and Scotland. Tufts of linear 2-in. leaves submerged; the slender flower spikes bear small pale lilac flowers and stand 1–1½ft. out of the water. A depth of 6in. of water is adequate.

L. fulgens. Similar to *L. cardinalis* but with larger flowers and not so hardy; it is usually treated as a half-hardy perennial, lifted for the

---

V. *Nymphaea marliacea* 'Chromatella'. Easily grown and very floriferous. For the larger pool

winter, but I know of plants of the cultivar L. f. 'Bee's Flame' which have wintered in 4–5in. of water without other protection. The beetroot-tinted foliage and crimson-scarlet flowers in 3-ft. spikes make this well worth trying.

L. paludosa. Swamp Lobelia. North America. Attractive spikes of pale blue flowers, 1–4ft. high. Shallow water. Propagated from seed, division or cuttings.

Ludwigia (Onagraceae)

Creeping, aquatic or bog plants useful for furnishing pond margins, some species used in aquarium planting. The majority have insignificant flowers.

L. palustris. Water Purslane. Southern Britain, North America. Found in acid pools, the stems creep along the soil under water, emerging or floating later. Opposite, broadly elliptical, glossy green foliage, red stems.

Lysichitum (Araceae). Bog Arum, related to Skunk Cabbage

L. americanum (at one time confused with *L. camtschatcense*). Rather a splendid plant for the bog or in shallow water. In early spring the large, 9–12in., acid-yellow spathes emerge, shortly followed by the enormous leaves, 2ft. long, which are waterproof so that raindrops run off them like quicksilver. Requires a deep soil. 1–1½ft., always wet or covered with 2–3in. water.

L. camtschatcense (syn. *L. japonicum*). Beautiful, pure white spathes 12in. tall, freely produced in early spring when this plant is perhaps the most conspicuous plant we have for the waterside. The enormous leaves follow and the green spadix elongates bearing the many seeds. The latter provide the best means of increase, germinating easily; lifting the plants intact is a terrible job. Seedlings require four years to reach flowering size.

Menyanthes (Gentianaceae)

M. crista-galli (syn. *Nephrophyllidium crista-galli*). Cock's-comb. North America. A large plant. The 2–4in. reniform leaves are borne on slender 1–2ft. stalks. It has cymes of fringed white flowers.

H

M. trifoliata. Bog-Bean, Buck-Bean, Marsh Trefoil. North temperate regions. Commonly found in mountain tarns, along streamsides and in marshy ground, this attractive plant has horizontal green rhizomes bearing olive-green trefoil leaves resembling those of the broad bean in texture. The flowers are fringed, white within, pink without, and the stamens are reddish; the short spikes appear 6in. above the water in early spring. The plant is happy in 1–12in. water. Propagate by division in spring.

Myosotis (Boraginaceae). Forget-me-not, Scorpion Grass, Mouse Ear

M. scorpioides (syn. *M. palustris*). Water Forget-me-not. Europe, Asia, North America. A British native, this is a fine plant for any water garden. The bright blue flowers appear in May on 9-in. stems taller in shade. Shallow water is best. Increases by seed very readily.
'Mermaid'. A recent introduction with larger, even more vivid, deep sky-blue flowers. Propagate from cuttings.
semperflorens. A more dwarf variety, flowering all summer.

Nymphoides. See **Limnanthemum**

Orontium (Araceae). Golden Club

O. aquaticum. A delightful and very handsome plant which needs rich deep soil. In shallow water the leaves stand out of the water, in deeper water they float on the surface. They are lanceolate, acute, dark green with a waxy surface so that the water runs off them. When submerged, they appear to be silvery as a result of the tiny bubbles of air clinging to them. The flowers are condensed into a narrow spadix and are golden-yellow, with stems which are pure white near the spadix, greener below. Once established, it is very difficult to move and it should be propagated by seed, which is usually freely set. 2–6in. depth of water is required and 1–1½ft. of loamy soil.

Peltandra (Araceae). Arrow Arum
P. alba. White Arrow Arum. Handsome plant for the pool

margin in shallow water, but deep soil. Broad, arrow-shaped
leaves on stems 8–18in. tall. The inflorescence is a 3–4in. white
spathe enclosing the spadix, which later in the year bears red berries.
Divide (with difficulty) in spring.
P. virginica (syn. *P. undulata*). Green Arrow Arum. Handsome
foliage, narrowly sagittate bright green leaves on long stems,
1½–2ft. tall. The inflorescence is of little account; the green spathe
is slender and I have never seen it open. The peltandras are all deep
rooting and need deep loamy soil. Shallow water or bog.

Penthorum (Saxifragaceae)

P. sedoides (syn. *P. sinense*). Jacob's Coat, Ditch Stonecrop. North
America. A semi-shrubby plant of no great moment until autumn,
when it develops a bright crimson hue. Spikes of greenish flowers
appear in late summer on 2ft. high stems. Shallow water or bog.
Propagate from cuttings.

Pontederia (Pontederiaceae)

A valuable genus for the water garden.
P. cordata. Pickerel Weed. North America. An indispensable plant
for shallow parts of the pool. The smooth glossy cordate leaves,
three times longer than they are broad, are sufficient in themselves,
but towards the end of summer when the closely packed blue
flowers are produced in short spikes above the foliage, this becomes
one of the best hardy aquatics. Height is 1½–2ft. 2–3in. of water
over 6in. of good soil is required. Other species need winter protection in Britain.

Potentilla (Rosaceae)

P. palustris (more correctly, but less well-known, as *Comarum
palustre*). Purple or Marsh Cinquefoil. Europe, Britain, North
America. Commonly found in wet bogs in northern Britain, this
rather rampant plant is not of great garden value except perhaps
for the wilder water garden, where its glaucous foliage and smallish, deep reddish purple starry flowers may be of some interest.

Preslia (Labiatae)

P. cervina (syn. *Mentha cervina*). Australia, Western Mediterranean. Allied to the mints. While not a showy plant, the foliage is sweetly aromatic, and it has 1ft. leafy spikes of lavender-blue flowers in summer.

'Alba'. Similar, but the flowers are creamy white.

Ranunculus (Ranunculaceae)

R. *lingua grandiflora*. A handsome variety of the common Spear-wort, but very much larger in flower. This is a fine plant where space is unlimited, but must be confined in a solid-sided container in the medium pool. The thick, succulent reddish stems bear attractive, smooth, deep green narrow leaves and heads of large buttercups, each rather more than 2in. wide on 4–5ft. stems. The fat white, creeping stoloniferous roots chase around a large pool in a very short time. Propagation is by division.

Richardia. See Zantedeschia

Rumex (Polygonaceae). Dock

While the majority of the dock family are too weedy for the garden, there is one species of some value for landscape effect by large lakes.

R. *hydrolapatham*. Great Water Dock. This large, strong-growing species, with stout, dark green 'dock' leaves, adopts brilliant crimson autumn colouring which can be very effective in the shallow margins of large lakes and water courses. The immense flower spikes should be removed before seed is shed, for it will germinate without fail and might constitute a menace.

Sagittaria (Alismataceae). Arrowhead

A useful race of aquatics for planting in 3–6in. of water, with handsome foliage and flowers.

S. *graminea*. Snow-white flowers in late summer, slender habit. 2½ft. The foliage is not, or very rarely sagittate.

S. *latifolia* (syn. *S. variabilis*). Duck Potato. A variable North American species, a few inches to 3ft tall, with foliage usually broadly arrow-shaped, the basal lobes as long as the blade. Pure

white flowers 1in. across are produced in late summer, and the
foliage often colours well in autumn. Spread is by means of
'turions', a kind of tuberous winter bud formed at the ends of the
slender underground runners.

flore pleno (syn. *S. variabilis fl. pl.*). Double flowers.

S. japonica. Regarded as a synonym of *S. sagittifolia* in some
quarters, for garden purposes it is very distinct and so is kept
separate here. The large, triangular sagittate leaves are a rather
dull green, and the large snow-white flowers very freely produced.
2½ft. is its height.

'Plena'. An indispensable water plant, the snow-white flowers
are so fully double as to be spherical, not unlike double stocks.
It is not rampant. Also 2½ft. tall.

S. macrophylla. Mexico. Large green leaves which colour well in
autumn. It is not reliably hardy, but will winter in mild districts if
the tubers are below the reach of frost. The flowers are white, and
it grows 3ft. tall.

S. sagittifolia. Common Arrowhead. Europe, Britain, Asia.
Spreads rapidly but is useful in the larger pool. Slender arrow-
shaped leaves with white male and female flowers produced
separately, the female ones being the lower. There is a dark violet
patch at the base of the inner perianth. Height is 1½ft.

Saururus (Saururaceae). Lizard's Tail

S. cernuus. American Swamp Lily. The upright 1½–2ft. stems bear
dark green cordate leaves and end in dense 6-in. spikes of nodding,
fragrant, small creamy white flowers, produced over many weeks.
Shallow water or bog conditions are suitable.

S. chinensis (syn. *S. loureirii*). China, Japan. The stout rhizomes
bear 12–15in. shoots of oval leaves, and 4–5in. terminal cylindrical
spikes of small, yellowish white flowers.

Scirpus (Cyperaceae)

The majority of scirpus species, and their allies cyperus and juncus,
are best suited to wild gardens where, in large colonies, they can
be very effective. For the medium and smaller water gardens there
are one or two species which are very good indeed. Being rather
invasive, they will require root restriction to keep them in order.

S. albescens. East Asia. This very effective plant produces stout rush-like shoots, sulphur-white in the early year, darkening to green as the year ages. Height is 4–5ft. It has an R.H.S. A.M.

S. holoschoenus (syn. *Holoschoenus vulgaris*). Atlantic Europe, Siberia. A rather rare native, best represented in the garden by its variety.

variegatus. A rather stiff habited, rush-like species, 1–3ft. tall, the stems banded horizontally in green and yellowish-white, alternately.

S. tabernaemontanii (syn. *Schoenoplectus tabernaemontanii*). Glaucous Rush. Britain, temperate Asia, Europe. Has produced from Japan one of the most striking waterside plants we have—

'Zebrinus' (syn. *Juncus zebrinus*). Zebra Rush, Porcupine Quill Rush. The 1½–4ft. stems are pure white, banded horizontally with green. 2–5in. depth of water is required.

Typha (Typhaceae). Reedmace

Erroneously known as Bullrush, which is really a scirpus. Large stands of typha make an impressive sight where there is a lot of space. The garden pool is not usually large enough to accommodate any except the most dwarf kinds, and even with these it is necessary to prevent undue spreading.

T. angustifolia. Lesser Reedmace. North America, Asia, Europe, Britain. The narrow, glaucous convex leaves grow to a height of about 4ft., the 'cats-tail' inflorescence has male and female portions slightly separated. It requires 1–6in. of water over 6in. of loamy soil. The rhizomes spread rapidly—6ft. or more in a season.

T. gracilis. A slender species, 3½–4ft., small brown 'cats-tails' in late summer.

T. latifolia. Great Reedmace. 6ft., a rampageous native far too strong-growing for the garden pool.

T. laxmannii (syn. *T. stenophylla*). South-east Europe to China. This is a much more manageable species, in which the very narrow semi-cylindrical leaves clothe the 3–4ft. stems. Male and female flowers are separated on the spike.

T. minima. The most useful and beautiful dwarf species, with narrow rush-like foliage and short, rounded, brown 'cats-tails' on 1–1½ft. stems. Although a miniature, the roots should still be con-

fined. It makes a good plant for a tub, or pig-trough water garden.
T. muelleri. New Zealand. In effect a slightly smaller *T. angustifolia*.

Veronica (Scrophulariaceae)

On the whole, the aquatic species are too rampant for use in the garden.

Villarsia (Gentianaceae)

Australian aquatics requiring protection.
V. nymphaeoides, see *Limnanthemum peltatum*.

Zantedeschia (Araceae). Calla, Arum Lily

Z. aethiopica (syn. *Calla aethiopica, Richardia africana*). South
Africa. Commonly grown as a cool greenhouse plant under the
generic name *Z. calla*, for the beautiful large white arum flowers
with a golden-yellow spadix. The white spathe is of kid-like
texture and the flowers are very fragrant. However, if the crowns
are planted in deep loam in about 9in. of water, they frequently
winter in average winters in a sunny sheltered pool. It grows 2–3ft.
tall. Or the roots may be lifted and stored in a frost-proof place
during the winter, replanting the following spring.

'Crowborough Variety'. A much hardier cultivar which may
be left in the pool all the year round, provided the crowns are
below the frost level. 1½ft. in height.

'Minor' (syn. 'Little Gem'). A smaller edition, 12in. tall, with
spathes 3–4in. long.

Submerged and Floating Water Plants

The establishment of a balanced pool in which vegetable and animal denizens live together, utilizing each other's waste products, is the ultimate aim of the water gardener, for when this state is achieved the water plants thrive, the fish are lively and the water remains clear indefinitely. Such a water garden will be a source of great pleasure for as long as the balanced state is maintained.

To achieve the balanced pool both animal and vegetable life is necessary; the animal part of the system is provided by the introduction of suitable freshwater fish, water snails and by smaller forms of animal life which appear in the water sooner or later, some from eggs introduced with water plants, some from aquatic insects which adopt the pool as a suitable home. My own pools were soon taken over as breeding places by the local toad population, and in March there was a steady procession from the surrounding fields, so that one had to take a torch out at night to avoid treading on the converging multitude. Oddly enough, there were no frogs to be seen for several years, until I introduced a few. I remember several years ago I was presented with tadpoles of the edible frog, and these went into the pool with all the other inhabitants, and were more or less forgotten, until two or three years later we were startled by hearing the adults giving song throughout the spring nights.

Animal pond life depends on dissolved oxygen for its survival, and excretes carbon dioxide as a waste product. This dissolves in the water and is taken up by the submerged vegetation as a basic food. The plants require carbon dioxide as a source of carbon in building up their new tissues, and in turn excrete the oxygen as a waste product. This dissolves in the water and becomes available for sustaining animal life in the water. This, of course, is an oversimplification of the complex interaction between plant and animal life, but it does explain the reason for planting oxygenating plants. While all submerged plants conduct this carbon dioxide-oxygen exchange, some plants are more efficient than others. A visible stream of pure oxygen bubbles may be seen issuing from a piece of the Canadian waterweed, elodea, submerged in a sunny pool. Without a constantly renewed supply of oxygen, animal life in a pool can use up the dissolved oxygen and ultimately create unhealthy conditions.

Other waste products from the animal partners are useful foods for the plants and, provided the balance is not upset, the water will remain healthy and clear. There is no need to give artificial foods to fish in an established pool, they will find quite sufficient natural food to maintain steady growth, and any excess of artificial food not taken at once will rot and create unhealthy conditions for fish and plants alike, upsetting the natural balance and fouling the water.

Floating aquatics are not particularly useful as oxygenators, but their often extensive roots are useful for removing excess nitrates from the water, and afford a shelter for small fish from the attentions of their larger relatives, as well as providing a change of diet for the fish. They are also useful in helping to keep water clear, and to some extent their shade discourages the growth of algae. Some are very attractive plants in leaf and flower. Planting them is merely a matter of dropping them in the water. The submerged aquatics may be planted in small containers in a little loam, or they may be planted in bunches held together by lead clips, or tied to a small stone, to sink them to the bottom of the pool, where they will soon establish themselves. Planting submerged water plants may be carried out at any time during the growing season, preferably before August, so that they may have time to establish and form resting buds to withstand the winter.

FLOATING AQUATICS

Azolla (Salviniaceae) Fairy Moss

A small group of plants more suitable for the aquarium than the outdoor pool.

A. caroliniana. Southern United States, tropical America. A charming fern-ally which increases rapidly by self-division, covering the pool with a moss-like carpet of soft green, turning red in autumn. An attractive plant for a small tub garden, but far too invasive for the larger pool where it will cover the surface, cutting light off from underwater plants so that they may die altogether.

Eichhornia (Pontederiaceae). Water Hyacinth

E. speciosa (syn. *E. crassipes*). Perhaps the most beautiful of all floating aquatics, this plant can be grown in the outdoor pool during the summer months, but must be wintered in a frost-proof place, potted up and kept moist, in a subdued light, until the following May, when it may be returned to the outdoor pool. In its native haunts in Africa, Australia and South America it is so prolific that it has choked waterways, and become a real menace to water transport. However, it will not stand any frost. It is well worth growing in the outdoor pool. The handsome, glossy leaves have greatly distended stalks which act as floats; the large flowers of lavender-blue are shaded purple, and have a large golden eye. The prolific roots hang down 12in. in the water, affording an ideal spawning medium for goldfish breeding.

major. A slightly larger variety.

Hydrocharis (Hydrocharitaceae). Frogbit

H. morsus-ranae. Europe (including England and Ireland), Asia. Usually found in calcareous districts in ponds and ditches, this is an attractive floating plant for the pool. The orbicular to reniform leaves, about 1½in. in diameter, are at first bronzed, later becoming bright green. The three-petalled white flowers are rather under 1in. wide. Towards autumn, stolons bearing winter buds (turions) are formed, which drop off and remain dormant until spring, when they rise to the surface and develop into plants.

Lemna (Lemnaceae). Duckweed

Several species throughout the temperate areas of the world. While some species may be useful to the aquarist, the pool owner should on no account introduce the surface species unless he is prepared to spend hours fishing them out at frequent intervals. They rapidly increase to form a dense carpet, excluding light from sub-merged plants which gradually give up the competition and die off. The only species which might be considered for the outdoor pool is the Ivy-leaved Duckweed, *L. trisulca*. The elliptic-triangular semi-transparent foliage—technically known as thalli—floats just below the surface. It has some oxygenating value and helps to keep water clear. Plants collected in the wild are likely to harbour organisms harmful to young fish.

Pistia (Araceae). Water Lettuce

P. stratiotes. This attractive but tender floating plant may be grown during the summer months out of doors, but must be wintered in a pan of soil with an inch or so of water, in a frost-proof place. The rosettes of pea-green, downy wedge-shaped leaves are about 6in. across, and the long white feathery roots hang down in the water. It grows best when the roots can reach soil, and it requires soft water to succeed. Throughout the tropics.

Riccia (Ricciaceae)

Aquatic relative of the liverworts, not recommended for out-door pools because of its rampant habit, but popular with aquarists.

Stratiotes (Hydrocharitaceae). Water Soldier

S. aloides. Europe, North-west Asia. This plant spends most of its time submerged, but rises to the surface at flowering time from June to August or, occasionally, because of the calcium content of the foliage. The rosettes of rigid spiny-toothed leaves are aloe-like. The white flowers are about 1in. wide, and the male and female flowers are borne on separate plants. There is a reddish-leaved variety called *purpurea*. It prefers calcareous waters in nature.

Trapa (Onagraceae). Water Chestnut

Several species of tender annuals which can be grown in the out-door pool during the summer months; the seeds are large, winged, nut-like objects.

T. natans. Rosettes of triangular, dentate leaves float by means of the swollen leaf-stalks, which are rose tinted. It is becoming very rare in nature; the seeds are available as a rule. They should be dropped into the water in May. Seed seldom sets in this country.

SUBMERGED AQUATICS

There is a vast number of submerged aquatic plants, but the great majority of these are more interesting to botanists than gardeners. However, there are a number of indispensable species which are valuable for their property of issuing considerable volumes of oxygen during the hours of sunlight, replacing that used up by fish and other water animals. A pool well stocked with submerged aquatics generally keeps fairly free of algae, that bugbear of the garden pool. A flourishing underwater planting competes successfully for available food with the filamentous algae. The foliage affords suitable spawning grounds for fish, and shelters the young fry from the cannabalistic tendencies of their parents.

Apium (Helosciadum) (Umbelliferae)

A. inundatum. Europe, to Russia, Italy, Tunisia. A local native water plant. The submerged leaves are finely divided, the aerial leaves pinnate. Small umbels of white flowers in July. Pretty foliage but not a particularly good oxygenator.
A. nodiflorum. A widely distributed species; the aerial foliage resembles watercress, and may attain 3ft. above water.

Callitriche (Callitrichaceae). Starwort

A large genus widespread throughout the world, the majority not in cultivation. For our purpose, we may consider our own native species, which grow freely and oxygenate well.
C. autumnalis. Useful in that it remains active during the winter months. Translucent pale green leaves carpet the mud and become darker as they age. The flowers are of no account.
C. verna. Small rosettes of bright green leaves on slender stems form a dense carpet on the pool bottom. It is an excellent oxygenator and food for fish, but too rampant and difficult to thin out to be trusted in the larger pool, and best confined to small tub gardens. It is useful for the aquarist.

Ceratophyllum (Ceratophyllaceae). Hornwort

Excellent oxygenators, never reaching the surface.
C. demersum. Brittle, freely branching stems bearing densely
whorled foliage, dark green. Will grow well in deep water, when
the growth may be from 1–3ft. long. Flowers inconspicuous.
C. submersum. Very similar but lighter in colour, softer in texture
and lacking spines.

Chara (Characeae). Stonewort

Very rampant and not recommended.

Elodea (Anacharis). (Hydrocharidaceae). Canadian
Pondweed

E. canadensis. An excellent oxygenator but should not be introduced to the larger pools, where it may be troublesome to control.
It rapidly increases, rooting into the pond bottom and forming
masses of slender stems thickly clothed with dark green oval leaves.
At one time this plant was a menace in our canal systems, but
suddenly calmed down after a few years' rampaging.
    crispa. Not reliably hardy, the strongly reflexed leaves densely
    clothe the long trailing stems and make it an attractive under-
    water plant, not too rampant and a good oxygenator. It can be
    overwintered in an aquarium.
    densa (syn. *Egeria densa*). An excellent oxygenator, the stems,
    densely clothed with narrow leaves, extend several feet in a
    season, but usually do not become embarrassing.

Fontinalis (Fontinaleae). Willow Moss
True aquatic mosses, these are best suited to running water, or
aquarium cultivation, and they seldom persist very long in the
outdoor pool.

Hippuris (Hippuridaceae). Mare's-tail.

Too rampant for garden use.

Hottonia (Primulaceae). Water Violet

H. palustris. Easter Britain, North Europe to Siberia. This charming native plant is a good oxygenator, with bright green, finely divided leaves, and spikes of soft lilac flowers in whorls at midsummer. It requires careful planting.

Isoetes (Isoetaceae). Quillwort

A genus of 'cryptogamic' plants, of which two British species are found in mountain tarns and lakes, usually in acidic waters, forming dense tufts of succulent leaves, a favourite food of fish.
I. echinospora. Britain, Europe from Italy to Iceland, Greenland. Tufts of rather flaccid, pale green leaves, 2–5in. long, growing in a stony peat in waters of low food content. Several forms.
I. lacustris. Similar distribution. Dense tuffets of stiff green tubular leaves, 6–9in., growing naturally in stony silt, in 1–1½ft. of water.

Myriophyllum (Haloragidaceae). Water Milfoil, Featherfoil

A family of useful oxygenators for pondkeepers, and also for furnishing aquaria. Of the many species our own native ones are as good as any of them for oxygenating.
M. spicatum. Whorls of rather dark green, bronzy, finely divided foliage, especially suitable for calcareous waters.
M. verticillatum. Brighter green, this very rapidly growing oxygenator also prefers calcareous waters; the finely divided foliage is attractive as well as efficient. When the myriophyllums have grown more than is desirable, it is simple to rake out the excess. The long stems tend to become leafless as they get older, and in this case the younger leafy sections can be cut off and replanted as cuttings, the older parts removed.

Oenanthe (Umbelliferae). Water Dropwort

Although *O. phellandrium* is a fairly good oxygenator, the dropworts are very poisonous and are better excluded from the garden pond.

Potamogeton (Potamogetonaceae). Pondweed

A large race of submerged aquatics, the majority are too rumbustious for the garden pool, taking charge and overhelming more desirable plants. There are a few species which are admissible if kept under control.
P. crispus. Densely set, wavy-edged green to bronzy red leaves, 3–4 in. long, it is an attractive species and a fairly good oxygenator.
P. densus. Densely set, green, tapering leaves.
P. pectinatus. Extremely slender stems and foliage, this is a good oxygenator, but requires keeping under control. It will grow well in deep water.

Ranunculus (Ranunculaceae)

R. aquatilis. Water Crowfoot. Britain, Europe, North America. This attractive native plant is a good oxygenator and it has finely divided underwater foliage, three-lobed floating leaves, and attractive white flowers. This plant grows well in running water, but may spread too much in the garden pool, especially if it is allowed to seed.

Tillaea (Crassulaceae). Pigmy-weed

T. recurva. Australia. Although of annual habit, this is an excellent oxygenator, adaptable to various depths of water, forming mats of narrow, dark green leaves up to 1in. in length. Usually it persists during the winter months, planted below the frost level. It is useful in maintaining clear water when growing well.

OXYGENATORS FOR THE HEATED POOL

Warm water holds less oxygen in solution than cold water, so the introduction of suitable submerged plants will assist in maintaining a healthy pool for the tender aquatics. Already mentioned are the floating eichhornia, and pistia, which will do extremely well in the heated pool. In addition there are several other floating plants which may be mentioned.

Ceratopteris (Ceratopteridaceae). Water Fern

C. pteridoides. Floating Fern. South America. The rosettes of broad, waved, floating fronds support the erect, much more divided, fertile fronds. The feathery roots, 9–12in. in length, hang down in the water, affording shelter to fish fry, and helping to absorb excess nitrogenous salts from the water,

Limnobium (Hydrocharitaceae)

L. stoloniferum (syn. *Trianea bogotensis*). A tropical frogbit, the ¾-in. diameter, orbicular leaves are dark green and float by means of spongy tissue on their lower surfaces.

Phyllanthus (Euphorbiaceae)
Natives of the tropics

P. fluitans. A charming floating plant, the small orbicular over-lapping leaves are arranged alternately and change in colour as they age from bright crimson to an attractive shade of green. The fibrous roots are bright red.

Salvinia (Salviniaceae)

An aquatic fern ally. Several species with a strong family resemblance. Of annual duration, their broad two-ranked leaves are most attractive. The apparent rootlets are really dissected fronds. It is best to keep stock growing in pans of wet soil in a frost-free house. The following species are the ones most usually offered.
S. braziliensis. Pea-green leaves (fronds?) attractively clothed with a felt of silky hairs.
S. natans. The species most often grown, it has bright pea-green leaves, their undersides coated with glossy brown hair.

Of submerged plants for the tender water-lily pool, the following is but a selection from the many species to be found in the warmer waters of the world. The majority of these are not grown by commercial growers, and in fact many of them are of botanical interest only.

10. *Primula frondosa*. Ideal for pondside planting in the small garden, with rosy lilac flowers and mealy leaves

Photograph by Ernest Crowson

11. *Iris pseudacorus* 'Variegatus'. Variegated-leaved form of our native yellow water iris, needing plenty of room either in shallow water or moist stream side

Photograph by Ernest Crowson

12. *Lysichitum americanum*. The brilliant yellow 'arum' flowers appear in April, followed by tropical-looking foliage. Thrives in shallow water or in bog but demands deep, rich soil

Photograph by Ernest Crowson

13. (*Above*) The hosta or Plantain Lily is invaluable for pondside planting for striking foliage effects   *Photograph by Ernest Crowson*

14. (*Above right*) Astilbe × *arendsii* 'Gladstone'. The astilbes are indispensable adjuncts to the water garden, thriving in any reasonably moist soil
Photograph by Ernest Crowson

15. (*Right*) *Iris laevigata*. The many beautiful cultivars of this truly aquatic iris give distinction to the garden pool   *Photograph by Ernest Crowson*

16. *Zantedeschia aethiopica*. The Arum Lily grows well in the sunny pool if the roots are planted below the reach of frost

Photograph by Ernest Crowson

17. *Caltha palustris* 'Plena'. The bright yellow double form of the Kingcup makes a splendid show in early March. May be grown in shallow water or in very moist soil near the pool

Photograph by Ernest Crowson

18. *Primula denticulata* One of the joys of spring. Thrives in any moist soil and varies from pure white, clear pink to deep blue in colour.

Photograph by Ernest Crowson

Cabomba (Nymphaeaceae)

C. aquatica. Mexico. Finely-divided, submerged foliage, reniform floating leaves. The sulphur-yellow flowers stand slightly above water level.

C. caroliniana. Fanwort. The most generally grown, this species is a good oxygenator. The submerged foliage, finely divided, is fan-like in outline, but the floating foliage is linear. The flowers are white. These plants are supplied usually as cuttings, and should be planted in small containers in loam. Occasionally available are the following varieties.

> *pulcherrima.* Has reddish purple stems, dark green divided leaves, and bright purple flowers.
> *rosifolia.* Stems and foliage are rosy red, and should be grown in a good light, to develop the full colour.

Cryptocoryne (Araceae)

A group of tropical aroids very popular as aquarium plants, needing fairly warm water; 70 °F. (21 °C.) suits most species. The inflorescence is usually reddish purple, standing well out of the water.

C. beckettii. Narrow, lanceolate, delicate green leaves, seldom exceeding 7in. in length.

C. ciliata. India. Growing about 12in. tall, this species has long, stout green leaves and fragrant flowers in a tubular, fringed spathe.

C. cordata. Malay. Yellowish green, wavy-edged cordate leaves, with a purplish reverse, and well marked veins.

C. griffithii. Malay. Crinkled, dark green linear leaves, purple flowers. It grows to 10in. tall.

C. nevillii. India. Uniform, green, lanceolate leaves, 1–3in. long.

Echinodorus (Alismataceae)

E. intermedius. Amazon Sword Plant. Brazil. Narrow, bright green translucent leaves, very decorative. Planted in 6–9in. of water. Foliage is produced above water level, and rosy white flowers. Spreads by means of runners.

E. macrophyllus. This has broad, spoon-shaped leaves with con-

I

spicuous veins. The white flowers are produced when the plant is grown in a good light.

Eleocharis (Cyperaceae). Hairgrass

E. acicularis. For those who would like an underwater lawn, this plant will produce a dense carpet of hair-like, bright green, 4–5in. leaves, when planted in loam. If it is decided to remove the plants, once thoroughly established, it will take some careful and lengthy labour.

Myriophyllum (Haloragidaceae)

M. hippuroides. America. Long shoots densely covered with hair-like leaves.
M. proserpinacoides. Parrot's Feather. A truly beautiful foliage plant from Buenos Aires. Planted in shallow water, the long trailing growths emerge from the water, clothed in lovely light green, finely divided leaves, the tips turning crimson later in the year.

Vallisneria (Hydrocharitaceae). Tape Grass, Ribbon Grass

Probably the most popular of oxygenators for aquaria, *V. spiralis* is of no great ornamental value for the heated pool, where the foliage is not conspicuous. It is an effective oxygenator and grows well in loam, spreading by runners to form a sward.

Hardy Plants for the Waterside

FERNS

Inasmuch as the successful water garden should be in full sun and the majority of ferns grow much more freely in shade, there are relatively few ferns which reach their full development in the correctly sited water garden. Nevertheless, several species will do well enough if they are planted in deep moist soil, enriched with leafmould. Their beauty of form and graceful habit make ferns highly desirable waterside plants. The following are recommended for waterside planting.

Adiantum pedatum

This hardy Maidenhair Fern is quite deciduous and will survive the most severe winters in Britain. Native of N. America, where it grows as far north as Alaska, this beautiful fern loves a moist position in humus-rich soil. The fronds brown easily in full sun but given the slight shade of taller plants, or under the arch of a bridge for instance the lovely fronds are a delight all summer. There is a dwarf variety from the Aleutian Isles, and a Japanese form with bright copper foliage in spring.

Athyrium filix-femina. Lady Fern

Although growing larger in shade, the lady fern and its many varieties will be most attractive if planted in moist deep soil; the tender, green fronds arch gracefully, and stand up well to exposure though not attaining their full stature. The plumose varieties (*A. f.-f.* 'Plumosum' in several forms) will not stand full sun, and should not be tried. A native, this fern has almost circumpolar distribution.

Dennstaedtia punctilobula

This has very finely-divided fronds rising at intervals from a creeping rhizome. Not a crown-forming fern, this North American species is not unlike the Lady Fern in frond shape.

Dryopteris

D. filix-mas. Common Male Fern. The wild type is perhaps too coarse for the pleasure garden, but some of the varieties are elegant enough for the choicest positions.

> *bollandiae*. The plumose male fern is much more finely divided than the type, and also assumes an attractive autumn colour when the deciduous fronds are dying down.

> *linearis*. An extremely refined variety, very slender frond divisions (pinnae) and surprisingly tough. It grows 2–3ft. tall.

> 'Grandiceps'. A superbly crested cultivar.

D. goldieana. This North American species has strong, pale golden-green fronds, turning all-gold in autumn. Deep rich moist soil.

D. pseudo-mas (syn. *D. borreri*). Golden-scaled Male Fern. This fern is a splendid sight in our Lakeland valleys in spring, the golden-green fronds are well set off by the thick clothing of orange-brown scales. It often grows in full sun but is larger and deeper green in shade. There are some fine crested varieties.

Matteuccia struthiopteris (syn. **Struthiopteris germanica**). Ostrich Feather Fern

A very handsome, moisture-loving fern producing symmetrical shuttlecocks of long, pale green fronds up to 3ft. high. Increasing by underground stolons, in time this fern covers a good deal of ground. Recently I visited a lake on the shores of which I planted a dozen or so in pre-war days, to find a colony covering some 700sq. ft. today.

Onoclea sensibilis. American Sensitive Fern

The ideal waterside fern, loving wet soil. In America it is regarded as a nuisance, However, it is such a lovely shade of pea-green, and the fronds so delightfully shaped, that it is welcome in most gardens. It spreads readily by branching underground stolons. Height is 1–2ft. in general.

Oreopteris limbosperma (syn. **Thelypteris limbosperma**). Mountain Buckler Fern

This British species loves a wet acid soil where its yellowish green, lemon-scented fronds stand up well to sunshine and may be anything from 1½–3ft. high.

Osmunda regalis. The Royal Fern

The most magnificent waterside fern, particularly if its roots can reach water, when it may attain 6ft. in height (much more in favoured natural habitats). The delicate pale green spring growth darkens as the year ages, finally adopting bright yellow to russet autumn colour. The fertile fronds are conspicuous when over-ripe, resembling the dead flower heads of an astilbe.
O. purpurascens. A glorious sight in spring when the coppery pink young fronds stand erect, purple-stemmed. A fine feature round the lake at Ness gardens in the Wirral.

The North American osmundas, *O. cinnamomea* and *O. claytoniana* are wonderfully handsome plants, preferring slightly acid conditions in deep rich swampy soil, but needing more shade than our native 'Royal'.

Woodwardia areolata. North American Chain Fern

This likes a rich deep swampy soil on the acid side. The sterile and fertile fronds are distinct, as in the next species. Height is 1–2ft.; fronds are smooth and pinnatifid.
W. virginica. Similar but with glaucous green fronds. It grows 1½–2½ft. tall.

HARDY HERBACEOUS WATERSIDE PLANTS

The ground around an artificial pond is not, in fact, likely to be any damper than the rest of the garden, but for planting round the shores of natural pools and small lakes where there is a high water table, there are many herbaceous plants which need the moist conditions to attain their best.

Anagallis (Primulaceae)

A. tenella. Bog Pimpernel. A native creeping plant always in saturated ground when found. Dense carpets of small leaves, pale pink flowers. A good carpeter for pond edges.

Anemone (Ranunculaceae)

A. rivularis. Fine for naturalizing around the larger pool, it bears open umbels of white flowers with violet stamens on 2-ft. stems. *A. virginiana.* Greenish white flowers 1½in. wide, hairy foliage.

Aruncus (Rosaceae). Goat's Beard

A. sylvester (syn. *Spiraea aruncus*). A massive plant producing 4–5ft. stems of drooping, white plumy flowers.
    kneiffii. Similar except that the foliage is finely laciniated.

Aster (Compositae). Michaelmas Daisy, Aster

There are several moisture-loving asters, including the many hybrids of the novae-angliae and novi-belgii sections. There are so many named cultivars that it is best to visit a nursery and choose colours for oneself.

Astilbe (Saxifragaceae)

Indispensable streamside plants. Often confused with spiraea, the latter usually have flattish heads of flowers quite different to the slender spires of astilbe. All the astilbes like very damp conditions during the growing season and grow well in almost any soil.

A. × *arendsii*. A group of hybrids of all shades of pink, mauve and red, as well as pure white. A glance through the lists of herbaceous plant specialists will afford a wide choice.

A. chinensis pumila. A valuable species which will cover the ground with deeply-cut foliage, and produce 18-in. spires of rosy purple flowers in August.

A. davidii. China. A distinct species used by hybridists freely, and well worth a place in its own right. Growing 4–6ft., the spires of fluffy, bright purple flowers often reach 2ft. long.

A. japonica. Japan. Plumes of white flowers, dark finely-cut foliage, up to 3ft. tall. Often grown for a cut flower.

A. rivularis. China, Himalaya. Deeply-divided foliage, spikes of creamy white flowers up to 5ft. in height.

A. simplicifolia. A dwarf 6–9in. Japanese species well suited to edge planting around the rock garden pool. Spires of dainty pale pink flowers over bronzed foliage.

Dodecatheon (Primulaceae). Shooting Star, American Cowslip

A race of moisture-loving American plants with cyclamen-like flowers in umbels on long slender stems. They die down early in summer and their positions should be marked in case they are disturbed when dormant.

D. dentatum. A rare species, consisting of rosettes of shallowly-toothed foliage and creamy ivory flowers, with a pointil of dark purple stamens.

D. hendersonii. Foliage 1–3in., pale purple flowers borne on 12-in. stems.

D. integrifolium. Elliptic, dull green leaves, 3–5in., with deep purple flowers on 9–12in. stems.

D. meadia. A strong-growing species, the pale lilac to magenta-purple flowers are borne on 12–24in. stems. There are several selected colour forms offered under such names as 'Brilliant', 'Red Wings', and so forth.

There are several other species with a strong family resemblance.

Epilobium (Onagraceae). Willow Herb, Fire Weed

A large family, some members very showy, but too ready to take charge to be admitted to the garden.

Euphorbia (Euphorbiaceae). Spurge

E. palustris. This handsome plant is not as well known as it should be; the glaucous foliage on 3-ft. stems is capped in May and June with large flat heads of glowing greenish yellow 'flowers'. The strong roots revel in moist lakeside soil.

Filipendula (Rosaceae)

Formerly attributed to the genus *Spiraea*, this group of handsome herbaceous perennials thrives in moist rich soil. The majority are better suited to the larger water gardens and to riverside and lake-side planting.

F. palmata (syn. *Spiraea digitata*). An easily-grown plant with narrowly-lanceolate, deeply-divided foliage and heads of light pink flowers at midsummer, on stems 1½–2ft. tall.

'Nana'. Under this name is a first-class plant for the rock garden or by the smaller pools. Usually listed under spiraea, it has a rosette of ground-hugging leaves and flat heads of fluffy rosy red flowers on 9-in. stems in July.

F. purpurea (syn. *Spiraea palmata*). Forms leafy bushes crowned with flat heads of crimson flowers on 3–4½ft. stems.

F. rubra. Better known under its older name, *Spiraea venusta*, especially in its cultivar 'Magnifica' which grows up to 6ft. tall and bears large handsome heads of rosy pink in June and July.

Geum (Rosaceae)

A group of perennials, one of which likes moist conditions, and is quite attractive in its cultivar.

G. rivale 'Leonard's Variety'. An improved form of the rather weedy native water avens; the flowers are of a rather attractive buff-pink. Height is 12–18in.

Gillenia (Rosaceae)

G. trifoliata. Indian Physic. A charming American plant with green spiraea-like foliage. The hard, slender, dark-coloured 2-ft. stems bear sprays of pretty, irregularly-shaped white flowers, with a touch of red.

Gunnera (Gunneraceae)

Brazil. The gunneras provide the largest leaves of any garden plants; a well established plant of *G. manicata* has been known to produce leaves 10ft. across, on 7-ft. stems, large enough for half a dozen people to shelter from rain under one leaf. They require deep, rich moist soil. The most imposing waterside plant for the larger pools and lakes.

G. chilensis (syn. *G. scabra*). When well established, it has leaves up to 4 or 5ft. across on 3–6ft. prickly stems, making a large mound of greenery. The small flowers are densely set on cone-like spikes up to a foot long, 4–5in. thick. Protect the crowns in winter by folding the foliage over the crown, and mulch thoroughly with compost or well rotted manure and leaves.

G. magellanica. A tiny creeper, compared with its big cousins, no more than 3in. high with 1-in. flower spikes. Quite hardy.

G. manicata. The giant of the family; when thoroughly established the leaves grow almost visibly during warm weather. In a well favoured situation the clumps may approach 12ft. high and 20ft. across. The flowering spikes are a rich golden-green and may be up to 4ft. high by a foot wide, though the individual flowers are quite tiny. The crowns should be protected in winter by folding the leaves over them. To obtain full development, the plants should be well mulched every year. The best planting time is late March or early April.

Hemerocallis (Liliaceae). Day Lily

Of recent years the day lilies have received a good deal of attention from the hybridists, and today there are described a hundred or more cultivars. The day lily is a superb waterside subject, revelling in deep, moist, rich soil, where the clumps of pale green linear leaves grow far too dense for any weeds to compete. They will flourish for years without attention, flowering freely all summer. Too many to describe, the reader is recommended to study the lists of specialists from which to make a selection.

Hosta (Funkia) (Liliaceae). Plantain Lily

Another indispensable group of perennials flourishing as waterside plants in deep, moist, loamy soil, and in great demand by flower arrangers for their attractive foliage. They should be allowed to grow into large clumps without disturbance, when they will give of their best. When required they may be lifted—with some effort —and divided in spring. The naming of hostas is rather chaotic but I hope not to have gone far astray with the following. They are all from Japan.

H. albomarginata (syn. *H. lancifolia albo-marginata*, *H.* 'Thomas Hogg', *H. decorata*). Dark green foliage with narrow white border.
H. crispula. Large, deep green leaves with conspicuous white edge.
H. fortunei. Large green leaves, lilac-mauve flowers on 1½-ft. stems.

albopicta. Bright yellow, green-edged leaves in spring, becoming an even green later.

'Aurea'. Large leaves evenly suffused with yellow.
H. lancifolia. Long-stalked, medium lanceolate, glossy green leaves, lilac flowers in late summer.
H. plantaginea. This has large, cordate, yellow-green leaves, and immense, pure white fragrant flowers on 1½–2ft. stems, a first-class plant not often seen, it flowers in August and September.
H. sieboldiana elegans. Large glaucous leaves, white flowers in June.
H. tardiflora. A small-growing, very late-flowering plant, light purple in flower, and reaching an all-over height of between 6 and 12in.
H. tokudama. One of the best foliage plants for the waterside. Intensely glaucous blue foliage, pale lilac flowers, on stems 1½ft. tall.
H. undulata. Twisted leaves freely striped with white variegation, one of the most attractive forms, lilac flowers in August on stems 9–12in. tall.

erromena. Forms large clumps of bright green leaves, broadly

ovate. Pale lilac flowers on 2-ft. stems in August. Not glaucous.
H. ventricosa. Narrow, dark green foliage, bluish purple flowers in
August on 1½-ft. stems, the darkest-flowered species. There is a
rare variety with golden-edged leaves very seldom seen.

Iris (Iridaceae)

This most valuable genus has many members eminently suitable
for lakeside planting. The majority have American or Chinese
origins, and mostly they are calcifuge. The main difficulty today is
to find the true species, for they interbreed freely in cultivation and
are raised readily from seed. On occasions I have submitted without success specimens of specially attractive qualities to our
botanic gardens for identification. Some of these hybrids are
better garden plants than the original species. Usually iris flowers
are evanescent, but they are a joy while they are out.
I. aurea. Himalaya. Large, rich golden flowers in late June, broad
sword-like foliage. 4ft. in height.
I. bulleyana. China. Grassy foliage, rich blue flowers in June. 2ft. in
height.
I. chrysographes. China. The flowers vary from almost black,
through light purple to reddish purple, and the falls are always
netted with bright gold veining. It flowers in June. Height is 2ft.
Tolerates some lime.
I. clarkei. Himalaya. A delightful dwarfish species, the bright
blue flowers are veined dark purple and appear in June on 9-in.
stems.
I. cristata. North America. A dwarf creeping species for the rock
garden streamside. Bright lilac flowers with orange blotch. 6in. in
height. There is a pure white flowered variety. Flowering-time is
May.
I. delavayi. China. This fine species may attain 5ft. when bearing
its brilliant violet-blue, white-spotted flowers in June.
I. douglasiana. California. More or less evergreen, broad green
leaves; the flowers are variable in colour from almost black to pale
blue, during May, and hybrids frequently appear amongst seedlings. 12in. is the height.
I. forrestii. A slender-growing, Chinese species, with grassy leaves
and attractive soft yellow flowers in June and July on 12–18in.
stems.

I. graminea. The very fragrant purplish flowers nestle modestly deep amongst the grassy foliage, 12in. tall. Flowering in May and June.

I. kaempferi, see Marginal Plants, p. 110.

I. laevigata, see Marginal Plants, p. 110.

I. pseudacorus, see Marginal Plants, p. 111.

I. sibirica. Europe. The species is overshadowed by the many named cultivars which are invaluable waterside plants. They spread dense mats of arching foliage in any good moist soil with added humus, and any plant specialist's catalogue will contain a good selection from which to choose. Height in general is 3–4ft. and flowering time is June and July.

Kirengeshoma (Saxifragaceae)

K. palmata. Japan. This very distinct plant flowers late in the year, September–October. The flowers are borne on purplish stems 2–4ft. high, and are bell-shaped, pale yellow and waxy in texture. The foliage is light green, deeply dentate and slightly hairy. It is propagated best from spring cuttings 4–5in. long. A deep, fertile soil containing plenty of rotted organic matter will ensure strong growth.

Leucojum (Amaryllidaceae). Snowflake

Of the several species of these bulbous plants, one thrives in wet soil and is even unharmed by occasional submersion.

L. aestivum. Summer Snowflake. Central Europe. Long strap-shaped leaves, clusters of large snowdrop-like flowers on 1–2ft. stems in summer.

Ligularia (Senecio) (Compositae). Giant Ragworts

Large robust plants admirably suited to lakeside conditions.

L. dentata (syn. *L. clivorum, Senecio clivorum*). China. Large rounded, glossy, light green leaves up to a foot across, branching stems of large orange 'daisy' flowers, July–September. 3–4ft.

'Desdemona'. A most impressive plant, the leaves are beetroot-red and the flowers a glowing deep orange. Other cultivars are

'Orange Queen' and 'Othello', both with deeper orange flowers than the type; the latter also has purple shaded leaves.

L. × *hessei.* Cordate foliage, yellow flowers on stems up to 5ft. tall. 'Gregynog Gold'. A compact free-flowering form. 3ft. tall.

L. hodgsonii. Roundish, serrate, purplish foliage through which thrust the 2-ft. stems topped by bright orange flowers in June–July.

L. japonica. Japan. Large foliage, deeply dentate. Tall stems of yellow flowers in June and July.

L. paludosus. Giant Fen Ragwort. Europe, Britain. A handsome plant which will grow either with the roots submerged or in deep moist soil. The foliage is lanceolate, serrate and downy beneath. Large heads of golden flowers in summer borne on stems up to 6ft. tall.

L. przewaliski. Mongolia. This very distinct plant is well worth a prominent position. Ground-hugging, deeply dentate, deep green foliage, from which spring slender spires of small orange-yellow flowers on almost black stems 5–6ft. tall. July is its flowering time.

L. smithii. Chile. Large, cordate, dark green foliage in dense mounds, over which appear conspicuous heads of 2-in. diameter white flowers. A good colony is a handsome sight at 2–4ft. tall.

L. veitchiana. China. Stout cordate foliage, leaves up to 16in. long. Branching stems of large golden flowers, 3–6ft. in height.

L. wilsoniana. China. Cordate, indented foliage, 3–5ft. spikes of small yellow flowers. A neat-growing plant.

Lythrum (Lythraceae). Loosestrife

Useful swamp plants for mass planting.

L. salicaria. British native. It has showy, reddish purple flowers on 3-ft. stems in July and August, but even so it does not compare with its cultivars.

atropurpureum. Rich dark purple flowers in dense spikes.

'Brightness'. Clear pink flowers on 3–4½ft. stems.

'Lady Sackville'. Bright rosy purple flowers. 3½–5ft.

roseum 'Perry's Variety'. Cherry-red flowers, larger than those of the wild plant.

'Superbum'. Clear rose flowers, often reaching 5ft.

'The Beacon'. Possibly the brightest, almost red flowers. Stems 4ft. tall.

Other cultivars are 'Dropmore Purple', 'Morden's Gleam' and 'Morden's Pink'; their names explain their colours.

L. virgatum. This species is more dwarf, with small leaves and more slender spikes which remain in flower a fortnight longer than those of *L. salicaria.* Cultivars in cultivation include 'Rose Queen', 2ft.; 'Robert', bright pink, 2½ft.; 'The Rocket', rosy carmine, 3ft. All lythrums may be propagated from spring cuttings which will make good plants for autumn planting.

Mimulus (Scrophulariaceae). Monkey flower

An ideal plant for pondside planting, providing a profusion of bright flowers all summer if the plants are prevented from setting seed. All are raised easily from seed or cuttings.

M. cardinalis. North America. This has light downy foliage, orange-scarlet flowers on 1-1½ft. stems from June to August. There is a pink cultivar called 'Rose Queen'.

M. cupreus. Bright coppery orange. Height 6-12in., with a rather tufted habit of growth.

M. lewisii. North America. A charming plant, with bright green, slightly downy leaves, and bright rosy crimson flowers on stems 1-2ft. tall.

  albus. A lovely plant, the pure white flowers and downy foliage make an exquisite combination.

M. luteus. North America, naturalized in Britain. It usually has clear yellow flowers, but in the variety *guttatus* they are spotted dark reddish brown. 1-1½ft. is the average height. There are a number of hybrids which should be kept going by taking cuttings in case the plants flower themselves to death; flowering is all summer from May onwards.

  'A. T. Johnson'. Large, rich yellow flowers, mottled maroon.
  'Cerise Queen'. Unspotted deep cerise, 9in. tall.
  burnettii. Large, brownish orange flowers, 9in. tall.
  'Red Emperor', 'Fireflame', 'Wisley Red' and 'Whitecroft Scarlet' are other cultivars amongst many, which stand out for vivid colouring, particularly the last—a dwarf form with vivid orange-vermilion flowers in great profusion; the plants seldom exceed 4-5in. in height.

M. moschatus. North and Central America, naturalized in Britain. The old Monkey Musk, grown for generations for its strong perfume which, mysteriously, suddenly disappeared. The plant we grow today is quite scentless, but is a pleasant little plant with downy, pale green foliage and soft yellow flowers on stems 4–5in. tall.

M. primuloides. California, Washington. A tiny mat-forming species, producing many bright yellow flowers on 2-in. stems. Seed should be saved as a precaution in case the tiny plants are heaved out of the ground by severe frosts.

M. ringens. North America. Soft, violet-blue flowers on slender 1½–2ft. stems, this is not a showy plant, but will actually grow in shallow water.

Monarda (Labiatae)

North American streamside plants with intensely aromatic foliage.

M. didyma. Oswego Tea, Bee-balm. Mat-forming perennial with heads of brilliant scarlet flowers. The cultivars are fine border plants for moist soils.

'Cambridge Scarlet', 'Croftway Pink' and the similar 'Melissa' explain themselves; 'Mahogany' purple-red, 'Mrs Perry' crimson, 'Pillar Box' scarlet, 'Prairie Night' deep purple and 'Prairie Glow' salmon-red, are amongst the most popular cultivars.

Petasites (Compositae)

Exceedingly rampant plants which are very difficult to eradicate once well established. It is better to leave them to botanic gardens on the whole.

P. japonicus. Striking lakeside subject, the leaves may reach 4ft. in diameter. It has white 'coltsfoot' flowers in February.

P. giganteus. May reach 6ft. in height and has even larger leaves. The tiny white flowers appear in dense heads before the leaves grow in spring. The boiled stalks may be used as a vegetable. These plants spread rapidly by underground runners, every broken piece of which will make a new plant, so be warned.

Peltiphyllum (Saxifragaceae)

P. peltatum (syn. *Saxifraga peltata*). The Umbrella Plant. California. This is a valuable streamside plant; the stout rhizomes creep over the ground, sending up immense, peltate leaves up to a foot across on 2–3ft. stems. The heads of palest rose flowers appear before the leaves in early spring on 2-ft. stems.

Podophyllum (Podophyllaceae)

P. emodii. Himalaya. Striking, three-lobed bronzy foliage very noticeable in spring, becoming light green with dark blotches. The white to pale pink flowers on 12–15in. stems give rise to large, egg-shaped scarlet fruits, 2in. long.

P. majus. Grows about 6in. taller, otherwise similar.

P. peltatum. Oregon May Apple, Lemon Apple, American Mandrake. North America. Pale green leaves turning bronzy orange, white flowers followed by yellow fruits about midsummer. Height is 18in. The leaves and roots are poisonous.

Polygonum (Polygonaceae). Knotweed

A race of, mostly, invasive weeds, although the following are worth having if kept under control. They ramp in any moist soil.

P. amplexicaule 'Speciosum' (syn. *P. a.* 'Atrosanguineum'). Spikes of bright scarlet flowers in summer on 2½-ft. stems. The species is from Himalaya.

P. campanulatum. Rather a lovely plant, mats of deeply veined downy leaves, branching heads of soft pink flowers. 3ft. in height. Those oriental species, *P. chinense*, *P. sacchalinense* and *P. sieboldii*, now attributed to the genus *Reynoutria*, should on no account be admitted to the small garden. I have been trying to rid my garden of them for thirty years and yet they appear. They have their place by a lake in a wild garden perhaps.

Primula (Primulaceae)

A vast race of over 500 species from all parts of the world, divided

---

VI. *Iris kaempferi* in its many cultivars is ideal for waterside planting where its roots can reach the water

VII. *Lysichitum americanum* flowers in late March and April. It needs plenty of space to develop it's enormous leaves

into several sections, and able to give the plant lover a lifetime of interest. All are beautiful and I think if I had to confine myself to one genus *Primula* would be the first choice. From the water garden context, only the Farinosae section, typified by our own birds-eye primrose, the Sikkimensis and the Candelabra sections, need concern us. All require a good deep soil with added humus, and mostly they are raised easily from seed, provided this is fresh.

Farinosae section.

The following are readily available:

P. farinosa. Birds-eye Primrose. Dainty heads of soft rosy lilac flowers in April–May over rosettes of white powdered leaves, 4–5in. long. Stems up to 12in. tall.

P. frondosa. Similar, but flowers twice the size and twice as easy. Height about 4–5in. on average.

P. gemmifera. Delightful. Small rosettes of bright green leaves, pale lilac flowers on 10-in. stems in spring.

P. involucrata. Dense rosettes of small, spoon-shaped, bright green leaves 2–3in. and pure white, fragrant flowers with a yellow eye on mealy 10-in. stems in May.

P. luteola. A much larger plant with basal rosettes of pea-green leaves, 4–12in. long, and soft yellow flowers in heads on 12-in. stems in spring.

P. rosea. Tufts of bright green leaves, 4–5in. long, intense carmine flowers in April. 5in. tall. Likes a wet position throughout the year.

'Delight' (syn. 'Visser de Geer'). A large flowered cultivar with brilliant carmine-pink flowers, May–June. 9 in. is the height.

Sikkimensis section.

P. alpicola. Hanging bells of soft ivory on 18-in. stems in May and June. There is a new race of coloured forms.

violacea. Similar, except that the violet-blue flowers, powdered with fragrant farina, strike a new colour note.

P. florindae. The Giant Himalayan Cowslip. Many-flowered heads of deep yellow bells on 2-ft. stems in June and July, this primula has large, ovate, long-stalked leaves. Naturalizes by self-sown seed. There is a copper-yellow-flowered variety now in cultivation.

P. secundiflora. Rosettes of bright green, pointed elliptic leaves 6in.

K

long and umbels of hanging, deep wine-purple bells in June, on 18-in. stems.

P. sikkimensis. Himalaya. A more refined version of *P. florindae*, more slender foliage, fewer but larger yellow flowers in May and June. Very fragrant. There is also a copper-yellow-flowered form.

Candelabra section. The flowers are in tiers.

P. aurantiaca. Bright orange flowers on red-tinted, 12-in. stems in July, bright green leaves. It requires careful cultivation.

P. beesiana. China. Bright purple, yellow-eyed flowers in tiers, 2 to 8 in number, on 18–24in. stems. Easy to grow and the parent of many fine hybrid strains.

P. bulleyana. Bright orange-yellow flowers in many tiers in June. One of the easiest species, reaching about 2ft. in height. A parent of many hybrid strains.

P. burmanica. Up to 6 tiers of reddish purple flowers with yellow eyes in June, green foliage with no farina. The stems are 2ft. tall.

P. chungensis. Vivid pale orange flowers in June on powdered stems, in 2 to 3 tiers. 2ft. is the height.

P. cockburniana. A biennial species with vivid orange-red flowers in 1 to 3 tiers on 1-ft. stems during June.

P. helodoxa. 4 to 6 tiers of bright yellow flowers. 2–3ft. in height. Flowering time is June. Collected by Forrest in Yunnan in 1912, this fine species should be in every garden where there is plenty of moisture.

P. japonica. This fine, well-known species ramps like a cabbage in any deep moist soil and may produce up to 6 tiers of purplish red flowers on 1½ft. stems in May–June. Easily raised from seed, there are several colour forms to be had, including a pure white.

P. pulverulenta. Another indispensable species, the flowering stems are densely powdered with white farina. Many tiers of rich purple flowers are produced in June on 3-ft. stems. Numerous hybrids and cultivars are available; we may mention the 'Bartley' strain, with pure pink flowers, and 'Red Hugh', bright vermilion flowers, which come true from seed if plants are not too near other species.

P. smithiana. Himalaya. Sometimes regarded as a variety of *P. helodoxa*, this species differs, however, in many details. The flowers are pale yellow in 1 to three tiers on 2-ft. stems in June. Must be kept moist throughout the growing season.

There are many other primulas which might be mentioned such

as *P. denticulata* and its many cultivars, but I find that this species is better with less saturated conditions; other primulas are not readily available except from a few specialists.

Ranunculus (Ranunculaceae)

R. aconitifolius. Europe. Dark green, palmately-divided leaves, and branching stems of white flowers, in May and June on 1½ft. stems.
  flore-pleno. Fair Maids of France. Very double, pure white flowers in profusion; this is a first-class plant for a moist, but not waterlogged, position.

Rheum (Polygonaceae). Rhubarb

Includes some magnificent foliage plants, with a striking inflorescence.
R. palmatum. Tibet. Immense deeply-cut, five-lobed leaves, tall panicles of creamy flowers. May reach 8–9ft.
  'Atrosanguineum'. More deeply-cut foliage, crimson flowers and fruits. A splendid plant for the large poolside.
The rheums are slow to establish and should be left alone to grow into specimen plants.

Rodgersia (Saxifragaceae)

Stout creeping rhizomes, conspicuous heads of fluffy flowers in midsummer. They require deep peaty soil which never becomes dry in summer.
R. aesculifolia. Large, deeply-divided horse-chestnut-shaped leaves up to 1½ft. wide and 3–4ft. sprays of white flowers.
R. pinnata. China. Dark green, divided foliage and branched stems of rosy flowers, 2–3ft. There is a pure white variety.
  elegans. A very fine plant, with bronzed leaves and rich rosy red flowers.
R. podophylla. Japan. Large, bronzed, palmate leaves and dense spikes of yellowish flowers.
R. sambucifolia. China. The bright green leaves resemble those of elder. Large panicles of creamy flowers are borne on 3-ft. stems.
R. tabularis. China. This very distinct species, sometimes referred to as *R. astilboides*, produces large, orbicular leaves 2ft. wide, pale

green on long stems. Heads of creamy white flowers, similar to those of astilbe, are produced in late June.

Sanguisorba (Rosaceae)

S. canadensis (syn. *Poterium canadense*). North America. Meadow-sweet foliage, tall stems, up to 6ft., of feathery white flowers.
S. dodecandra (syn. *S. vallistellinae*). Seldom seen species, but an acquisition. Much more slender than the last, with drooping fluffy white flowers on 3–4ft. stems.

Saxifraga (Saxifragaceae). See also Peltiphyllum

S. pensylvanica (syn. *Micranthes pensylvanica*). Swamp Saxifrage. North America. A thick creeping rhizome, large oval leaves and dense heads of greenish flowers make up a handsome plant, 2–3ft. tall.

Senecio (Compositae). See also Ligularia

S. pulcher. South America. A very distinct species with large, crimson-purple, yellow-centred flowers in late summer. It requires rich moist soil without lime. It is said to be quite hardy, but I have never succeeded with it.

Spiraea. See Filipendula

Trollius (Ranunculaceae). Globeflower

Europe, Asia, North America. Beautiful in foliage and flower, the globeflowers prefer deep moist soil near the water. Our native species, *T. europaeus*, is found alongside our northern rivers and often climbs high into the mountains.
T. acaulis. North India. A charming dwarf species seldom exceeding 4in. The lemon-yellow flowers are flat, not globular.
T. europaeus. Medium, soft yellow globular flowers on 1½ft. stems.
   albidus. A rare variety with creamy white flowers.

There are a good number of excellent hybrids or cultivars, with flowers from pale lemon to deep orange, and a perusal of any good catalogue will provide a wide choice.

T. ledebourii. Siberia. A fine plant with large, rich orange flowers on 3-ft. stems. The flowers are open saucers.

Uvularia (Liliaceae). Bell-wort

Requiring deep, humus-rich soil in slight shade, it has a habit similar to that of Solomon's seal (*Polygonatum*).

U. grandiflora. Bright green foliage, on stems 1-1½ft. tall, with hanging yellow bells. The slightly twisted petals are 1½in. long.

U. sessiliflora. It has pale yellow flowers, not so attractive as the last, but easier to make at home. It is more correctly, but awkwardly, known as *Oakesiella sessilifolia*.

Reeds, Grasses and Bamboos for Waterside Planting

To complete the water garden picture, some vegetation is desirable to contrast with the predominantly horizontal lines of water and water-lilies. There are no plants so well suited to this role as the various moisture-loving members of the great family of *Gramineae*, the grasses, and their relations, members of the family *Cyperaceae*. Although there is a tremendous choice available in these families, a great many of the species are too rampant, or not sufficiently distinguished to be chosen for garden adornment, but there are several most valuable subjects suitable for our consideration. When it is desired to grow some of the more rampant species, it would be wise to confine the roots in concrete pockets or containers, so that they cannot get out of hand.

Arundinaria (Gramineae). Bamboo

The bamboos are really woody grasses, mostly from Asia. Evergreen in their native haunts, they will require a very sheltered position if they are to retain their leaves in our winters, although some species will endeavour to remain evergreen. Cold winds are the chief enemy. Propagation is by careful division in early May. The majority of hardy species are far too invasive for the smaller garden, magnificent as they may be when there is adequate space. The following do not spread too rapidly.
A. murieliae. China. Evergreen, 8–12ft., forming a dense thicket of gracefully arching foliage. Stems green, finally yellow, the rich green leaves are from 2–4in. long.
A. nitida. A similar non-running species, except that the stems are

black, with small shiny leaves. One of the most graceful bamboos, growing 6–10ft. high. I have had a clump for over thirty years which has not exceeded 6ft. in width.

A. spathiflora. Although this species seldom reaches 10ft. in this country, it attains 20–30ft. in height in its native Himalaya. Evergreen and not spreading, it resembles the very rampant *A. anceps.* The leaves are 3–5in. long. A very graceful and elegant species.

Arundo (Gramineae). Reed

Needing abundant sunshine and shelter from cold winds, the 10–15ft. stems terminate in large plumy panicles. Abundant moisture is required, but not waterlogged conditions.

A. donax. South Europe. Ornamental glaucous foliage on stout stems which are strong enough to use as fencing.

A. macrophylla. Extra wide, dark green leaves.

Bambusa

There are no hardy species of *Bambusa*, the true bamboo. See *Arundinaria*.

Carex (Cyperaceae). Sedge

One or two species of this large group may be introduced for their graceful habit.

C. pendula. Europe, Britain, North Asia. Stout grassy foliage, arching 3–4ft. stems of drooping brownish spikelets.

C. pseudocyperus. Bright green, grassy foliage, drooping spikelets of dark green. Height is 2–3ft.

C. riparia (sometimes listed as *C. stricta*). North temperate regions. Best grown in its variegated variety, 'Bowles' Golden'. Rich golden foliage, 15in. tall. Requires a very wet situation.

Cladium (Cyperaceae). Twig Rush

C. germanicum (syn. *C. mariscus*). Tall, rushy species, 3–6ft., with saw-edged leaves. Pale brown florets.

Cortaderia (**Gramineae**). Pampas Grass

Magnificent South American genus. The plants should be placed so that their splendour can be appreciated without crowding. Propagate by division in April–May.

C. selloana (syn. *C. argentea, Gynerium argenteum*). Makes large clumps of arching, narrow, dark green, saw-edged leaves up to 6ft. long. The huge plumy, silvery-white inflorescence is held erect on 10ft. stems. Plant where there is a distant dark background, and near the pool, where it can be reflected. Plant in April–May.

   aureo-lineata. Now rarely seen, this variegated-leaved variety is much to be desired.

C. quila (syn. *Gynerium quila*). This species is on the borderline of hardiness and will require protection in cold districts. The more graceful, looser, lavender plumes may be 1½ft. long, on 6–8ft. stems.

Cyperus (**Cyperaceae**).

C. alternifolius. Umbrella Rush. Madagascar. Tender. May be grown in the outdoor pool during the summer in a pot, lifted and kept in the house as a house plant during the winter. Grassy umbrella-like heads of leaves on 1–2½ft. stems characterize it.

   gracilis. Madagascar. A more dwarf variety with heads of narrower leaves on 1½-ft. stems. Not hardy.

   variegatus. Stems and leaves are striped white, but it is apt to revert to the green form. Tender.

C. atrovirens georgianus. Brilliant green leaves, dainty brown florets. Best actually in 2–3in. water. 3–3½ft.

C. congestus (syn. *Mariscus congestus*). Handsome species requiring deep rich soil, always wet. Reddish brown spikelets. It needs plenty of room and grows to 2ft. tall. Although from the Old World Tropics, this species has wintered here several years in the open.

C. haspan. Tropical America, Europe, Asia, Australia. Relatively few reddish brown spikelets on 1–3ft. stems. Tender.

   viviparous. Slender 2-ft. stems bearing crowded heads of light green foliage rather like a miniature papyrus. Young plantlets grow from the 'mop-heads'. It is tender.

C. longus. Sweet Galingale. A decorative native species for pool or lakeside where its grassy tufts of foliage and 2–4ft. stems of reddish brown plumes strike a distinct note.

C. papyrus (syn. *Papyrus antiquorum*). Egyptian Paper Reed. May be grown out of doors during the summer, but must be transferred to a heated greenhouse for the winter. The stout polished stems carry handsome crowded heads of long, thread-like leaves on stems anything from 8–16ft. tall. It is probably best grown in tubs which enable the plants to be carried indoors in autumn without root damage.

C. vegetus. Chile. A hardy species with broad grassy foliage which persists throughout the winter. 2–4ft. in height.

Eriophorum (Cyperaceae). Cotton Grass

Easily cultivated bog plants, requiring saturated soil on acid side.

E. latifolium. North temperate regions. Broad, rough, flattened grassy leaves and white, dropping spikelets with purplish green scales. A pretty plant, 1–1½ft. tall.

E. polystachion (syn. *E. angustifolium*). Britain and north temperate areas. Tufts of shiny, grassy foliage, with round heads of silky, snow-white 'cotton' above 1-ft. stems.

E. vaginatum. Britain, Europe, North America. Stiff, 3-angled rough leaves, with heads of pure white glossy 'cotton'. 10–12in. tall.

Eulalia. See Miscanthus

Glyceria (Gramineae). Manna-grass

Several rampageous species for wild garden planting. If kept under control with confined roots, the following might be considered.

G. aquatica variegata (syn. *G. foliis variegatis*). A really pretty variegated waterside grass, 2ft. high, bearing handsome broad 10in. leaves, striped green, yellow and white, also suffused in early spring and autumn with a rosy flush. If not confined, the creeping roots will extend 4–5ft. per season.

G. canadensis. Rattlesnake Grass. North America. A very handsome species, with 2–3ft. stems bearing drooping panicles of numerous spikelets resembling Quaking Grass (*Briza* spp.).

Imperata. See **Miscanthus**

Juncus (Juncaceae). Rushes

A large genus of plants, most of which are not admissible to the garden. There are one or two which are of interest.
J. effusus spiralis. The Corkscrew Rush. An interesting variety of the common rush, the 1½-ft. stems are twisted in a corkscrew manner. Not invasive.
J. ensifolius. Dwarf tufts of iris-like foliage with heads of brown florets on 12-in. stems.
J. glaucus. Clumps of stiff, glaucous blue, 2-ft. leaf-like stems. Needs a saturated soil.

Miscanthus (Eulalia, Imperata) (Gramineae)

Allied to the sugar canes, these are tall perennial grasses with feathery panicles, making beautiful specimens. Best planted without close neighbours, so that their full beauty may be appreciated. The variegated varieties should be protected in winter with cut bracken or similar material.
M. sacchariflorus. Hardy sugar cane. Japan. Reedy stems 5–8ft. bearing panicles of silky florets.
   'Variegatus'. Prettily white-variegated foliage.
M. sinensis (syn. *Eulalia japonica*). Japan. Robust perennial grass reaching 5–7ft., the broad, dark green leaves, up to 2ft. long, have a conspicuous, median white stripe. The panicles are purplish.
   'Gracillimus'. Large brownish panicles on 5–6ft. stems, the very narrow leaves have a central white stripe.
   'Variegatus'. The leaves are striped white and the stems are green and white, suffused pink. Not so strong as the type.
   'Zebrinus'. The leaves are barred horizontally with yellow and green.

Phalaris (Gramineae). Canary Grass

P. arundinacea. North Hemisphere. The type is rather strong for the smaller garden, growing 2–5ft. tall, with broadish leaves and purple-tinted panicles.

'Picta'. Ribbon Grass. Gardener's Garters. Popular waterside
grass, pale green leaves striped with white, sometimes tinged
pink.

Scirpus (Cyperaceae)

Mostly too invasive unless the roots are confined. The best
kinds have been mentioned in the chapter on marginal plants,
p. 117.

Zizania (Gramineae). Wild Rice

A most desirable waterside or aquatic grass; though annual, it will
sow itself for the following year. Sow on soil under water from
3in. to 3ft. deep.
Z. aquatica. Vivid green, broad flat leaves, on very slender arching
stems up to 6ft. high. Large panicles of tiny flowers.
Z. caducifolia (syn. *latifolia*). Siberia. Fine symmetrical broad leaves,
on 3–4ft. stems, distinct stamenate and pistillate sections of inflorescence. It is not suitable for small ponds.

Fish for the Modern Water Garden

No pool can be considered to be properly furnished without a thriving community of fish, water-snails and the like. Not only do the fish supply a necessary partner in achieving the balanced pool which is so desirable, but they provide a never failing source of interest and beauty to charm old and young alike. I can think of few occupations more restful than sitting a while on a quiet sunny day by the poolside watching the ceaseless evolutions of colourful goldfish and golden orfe amongst the waterplants. I remember on one such occasion a shelduck appeared, proudly leading a string of offspring on their way down to the shore. They lingered a day with me, the fluffy ducklings darting about, ducking under the surface and bobbing up again yards away, apparently as dry and fluffy as before.

Perhaps the most important role of the fish is to keep down the larvae of midges and mosquitoes which can be such a pest on summer evenings. These insects will lay their eggs on any sheet of water large or small, and the myriads of wriggling larvae produced therefrom are perfect fish food and obviously are much relished by the fish. Before introducing any fish into a newly planted pool, two or three weeks should be allowed for the plants to get well rooted, the reason for this being that fish normally grub about in the soil and may loosen newly planted aquatics so that they are found floating about on the surface.

In very sunny weather in a new pool, when the water-lilies have not produced many leaves, fish will appreciate a little shade artificially supplied by floating one or two well weathered boards in the water until the water-lily leaves are well developed. Weathered boards are specified because new wood may exude poisonous substances into the water.

Before buying your fish it is as well to calculate how many your pool will sustain. The old rule that one should allow a gallon of water to an inch of fish is now considered unreliable. Furthermore, in the balanced pool, where animal and vegetable life balance one another, the amount of oxygen emitted from the plants varies widely in relation to light intensity, and in fact in a shaded pool, the plants may use up more oxygen than they release and so deplete the amount available to fish.

It has been established that the most important factor in relation to the number of fish which may be kept is the surface area of the water; the oxygen from the air dissolved in the water is constant for any given temperature. Pools with a moving surface created by waterfalls and fountains will absorb more atmospheric gases than a still pool. For still pools for cold water fish, 3sq. in. of surface to an inch of fish, excluding fins, is the upper limit, so allow about 10sq. in. of surface to each 3-in. fish you put in the pool. Fish will grow of course, but they are very adaptable and will adjust their growth to their environment. In warm pools for tropical water-lilies less oxygen is absorbed from the air and in this case 6sq. in. of surface area should be allowed to an inch of fish.

When a pool is well established there will be no need to give artificial foods to the fish as they will find all they need in the water in the form of algae, midge larvae and other natural foods, but in a recently constructed and planted pool some artificial food may be given, sparingly, of course, and not more than the fish will take up in a few minutes. As a change, chopped-up earthworms will be well received. But as soon as the pool is well established, say in two or three months, it should be quite unnecessary to supplement the natural foods to be found in the water. Nowadays, most proprietary fish foods are well balanced, and during the winter months very little indeed will be needed, for the fish are inactive and indeed almost dormant. However, in early spring it may be advisable to supply a little food until the natural foods become plentiful again with the renewal of growth in early summer. Overfeeding is the cause of more trouble amongst fish than anything else—I have always suspected that Julius Caesar was overdoing things when he fed intransigent slaves to his lampreys. It is, of course, quite possible to train fish to come to their owner at feeding time, and to respond to a bell when food is available, but any temptation to put on a regular show should be resisted in the interests of the fish.

Of the many kinds of fish which can be kept in good health in still pools, by far the most popular is the common goldfish, a hardy and easily tamed species and one which associates well with other fish. Closely related to the common carp, the goldfish has been kept in British pools over 300 years, and often attains a large size and a venerable age. It is very variable in colour, reddish gold, golden-yellow, pink and even black varieties being not uncommon. The goldfish has been cultivated by the Chinese, Japanese and Koreans for many centuries, and they have made selections from various sports until today there are many very distinct varieties to be had. While these 'fancies' do well enough in the outdoor pool during the summer months they are not so hardy as the common type, but they are admirable pets to keep in an indoor or heated pool with the tropical water-lilies, and therefore will be dealt with more fully in the list of recommended kinds for tropical water-lily pools (pp. 160–3).

FISH FOR THE OUTDOOR POOL

While there are many species of fish which can be kept in outdoor pools, a good many are inconspicuous, especially from above, and it seems sensible to mention only those kinds which are highly coloured and decorative. Many of the less showy species are also retiring in habit, and one may seldom see them from one year to the next. Apart from the common goldfish, one or two varieties of it which are quite satisfactory out of doors are the following:

THE COMET

Raised in North America, this variety has an elongated body and much elongated tail fin, very graceful, and a very swift swimmer, but also given to jumping out of the water in spring when it is as well to keep an eye on them in case they land out of the water.

THE SHUBUNKIN

Another very hardy variety raised in Japan about the beginning of the century. The scales are so fine that it appears scaleless, and it is very varied in colour, often being patched in various colours and may be red, black, blue, yellow-brown, purple or white or a combination of all or any of these hues. A pure blue shubunkin is regarded as a great acquisition and is priced accordingly.

THE GOLDEN ORFE

One of the best fish to keep in garden pools, the golden orfe is a streamlined active species which likes to swim in shoals. It is a long-lived and easily kept fish and one of the best for keeping down midge larvae. They are a delight to watch and are very seldom troubled with disease. If for any reason it is necessary to remove them to another pool, this should be covered with netting, for golden orfe seem to resent being moved to new quarters, and will try to jump out, especially when they have grown large. On one such occasion I lost a score or more of 9-in. fish—they were found lying dead around the pool to which they had been moved the previous day.

The silver orfe is similar in all respects, except colouration, and is equally hardy and attractive.

THE GOLDEN RUDD

An attractive creature which associates peacefully with other fish. The scales are of a coppery bronze, the fins bright scarlet and the eyes also are bright red.

GOLDEN TENCH

The common tench is green in colour, but its golden variety is very handsome. Unfortunately, it tends to spend most of its time on the pool bottom. Also known as the Doctor Fish, because of the slimy mucilage covering the body which other fish rub against, apparently as a means to rid themselves of some disorder or parasite. The golden tench will attain a large size and lives for many years.

HI GOI

Another member of the carp family and not unlike the common goldfish, except that it has two pairs of barbels instead of the usual single pair. It is also rather more slender and more active. The Japanese have bred many highly coloured and variegated forms rather like the shubunkin except that the hi goi are clearly scaled.

KOI

This is the latest product of the Japanese fish hybridists, and has only recently arrived in this country. Koi are carp-like fish of almost all colours of the rainbow, red, black, blue and mauve blotches, often on a white ground, and there is a truly gold variety which is highly prized—and priced. A shoal of these highly coloured creatures in harlequin hues really is an impressive sight and almost certainly this will be the pond fish par excellence in the future. Koi are being bred in this country now, and should be in sufficient numbers to be readily available in a year or two.

Several of the above fish will breed when large enough, and it is quite a sight to see several males chasing and shouldering the female around the pool encouraging her to discharge her eggs which they fertilize in the water. If there is plenty of submerged waterweed in the pool, some of the eggs may escape the attentions of the ever-hungry parents and eventually hatch out. At first, young goldfish are dark coloured, but after a year or so they adopt the golden hue of their parents. If it is desired to raise many fish, it is as well to remove the parents and other mature fish to another pool as soon as the eggs are shed. Then there will be a chance for the youngsters to develop, instead of furnishing meals for their parents. Other coldwater fish such as catfish, sticklebacks and sunfish are too quarrelsome to be allowed amongst the more easy-going denizens of the pool.

FISH FOR THE HEATED POOL

This heading conjures up visions of vividly coloured tropical fish flashing around the water-lilies in the heated pool, but the view from above of a tank of these gorgeous jewels of the fish world is very different to that seen broadside on through the panels of an aquarium. The brightest and most colourful tropical fish display most of their colour on their sides or fins, and from above they appear as so many slender, modestly coloured creatures designed to elude the questing eyes of their enemies. By far the most attractive fish for the heated pool are the fancy varieties of goldfish. Of the hundreds of species of tropical fishes which are available for aquaria, the following should do well and at the same time be visible from above: all the various Barbs of the genus *Puntius*, their large glistening scales reflect every shaft of light; the Guppies, of which there are numerous mutations and, while they seldom exceed 1¼in. in length, they scintillate in strong light, and the various coloured Platies (*Platypoecilus*) in gold, red and sunset shades.

The guppies and platies are livebearers, giving birth to minute, free-swimming fish, which however, are quickly eaten by their parents and other fish, unless special precautions are taken to preserve them. If the pool is well furnished with vegetation a few may survive to maturity. The barbs, which are allied to goldfish, lay eggs, usually amongst vegetation, and these hatch out in two or three days if they have not been eaten already. The only satis-factory way to bring up fish fry to maturity is to have separate tanks well furnished with vegetation for each species to lay their eggs, and move the fish back to their community tanks as soon as the eggs are laid. Then the fry can be watched and fed with suitable food until they are strong enough to fend for themselves. Foods recommended for tiny fish after three or four days' growth are hardboiled egg rubbed through a very fine mesh, the creamy liquid from boiled oatmeal, and infusoria. The last can be prepared by pouring boiling water on a handful of hay in a bucket, filling up to the brim with cold water, and standing the bucket in the shade for a few days, when the water will be found to be teeming with microscopic life. A pint of this liquid poured into the pool with the fry will provide food for a day or two. The bucket should be filled up each time some is used. When the fry get larger, water-fleas (*Daphnia*), make an excellent food. Dried daphnia usually can be had from aquarium supply shops. The reader who would like to take up fish breeding is recommended to join the local aquarists' society and consult some of the specialist literature such as Dr H. R. Axelrod's *Exotic Tropical Fishes* (T. F. H. Publi-cations (London) Ltd.) and *Goldfish Pools, Water-lilies and Tropical Fishes*, by Dr G. L. Thomas, from the same publishers. This very large subject is outside the scale of the present work.

Of the fancy varieties of the common goldfish, which are ideal subjects for the heated pool, the following will be found excellent and never-failing in interest.

THE CELESTIAL

This remarkable fish is so called on account of the pupils of the

L

enlarged eyes being placed on the tops thereof, so that they appear to be searching the heavens. The body is usually chunky and may be red, black, or mottled.

THE FANTAIL

Should have a short, rather tubby body, and the tail and anal fins should be double, but frequently the tail fins are united along the upper edge to form a fan. The fancier rejects the latter form, but from an ornamental point of view there is little to choose between them. The body may be red, gold, or multicoloured and, while fantails are not rapid swimmers, they manage to get along very well.

THE LIONHEAD (U.S. BUFFALO-HEAD)

A short round body, no dorsal fin, and has warty growths all around the head; these sometimes develop to such an extent that the gills are hampered in their work, and may even lead to suffocation. The tail fin is short, and often this variety has trouble in swimming in the proper position, sometimes travelling head down.

THE ORANDA

Another sport on the same lines, except that it has a dorsal fin; the tail fin is often long and flowing so that it swims quite well. The warty outgrowths normally are confined to the top of the head. Both lionheads and orandas are usually of the normal goldfish colour, though variants do occur.

THE TELESCOPE

Most often seen as the velvety-black telescopic moor, it is usually fantailed as well. It may grow to 10in. or more, and obtains its name from the large protruding eyes. Quite an active fish, this is the fishy counterpart of the pekinese dog. It can remain in good condition for many years, the eyes becoming larger with age. Various coloured forms occur, such as the multicoloured calico telescope, veil-tailed telescope and so forth.

THE VEIL-TAIL

Perhaps the most attractive variety ever raised. It has a short, deep, chunky body and a long, filmy, double tail, two or three times as long as the body, and all the other fins are long and filmy as well. The fins offer more resistance than assistance to swimming, so that the fish appears to waggle its way through the water rather than to swim, rather like a plump, overdressed dowager at a party. However, I must confess to a weakness for this variety, it has a kind of majestic grace. The fins take two years or more to reach their full development, and then it is wise to reduce feeding gradually to half the normal rate, for overfeeding leads to deterioration and splitting of the fins. When a veil-tail occurs with but a single tail-fin it is known as a Nymph, and usually the fins are not so well developed. It is, however, a very graceful member of the group and is an active swimmer. Veil-tails may be any colour from black to bright red, or may be multicoloured.

WATER SNAILS AND SCAVENGERS

No pool can be considered complete without a few water snails. I have already warned the pondowner against the freshwater whelk, *Limnaea stagnalis*, which almost certainly will arrive, sooner or later, as eggs on some water plant, even if not introduced deliberately. This creature has a long pointed shell and breeds at an enormous rate, depositing its eggs in long, sausage-shaped, transparent masses about ¼ in. thick on the underside of water-lily leaves and other plants. It must be kept away from choice plants, and every effort made to eradicate it. Bait in the form of cabbage stalks will float on the water and attract numerous water snails overnight, and the limnaeas should then be removed and disposed of daily. It may not be possible to eliminate all of them in this way, but it should be possible to keep their numbers down to reasonable limits.

If any of the flat-coiled planorbis snails are on the bait, these should be returned to the pool, for this species is a most welcome and excellent scavenger, cleaning up waste animal products, dead insects and small algae. The egg masses of planorbis are flat, plate-like bodies, transparent, but tougher than the cylindrical egg masses of limnaea. Of the various species of planorbis, *P. corneus* is the one most often seen, the ramshorn snail. It occurs in black-bodied and red-bodied varieties, the latter, while just as useful in the outdoor pool, is also valuable and colourful in the aquarium. The freshwater winkle, *Paludina vivipara*, has a roundish shell, provided with an operculum or lid, with which it can close the shell against enemies. The body is black and yellow spotted. It produces its young alive, and confines its activities to scavenging decaying vegetation.

The freshwater mussel is a very efficient scavenger, but as it spends its time ploughing through the mud and may uproot plants it is a mixed blessing. Also, it has a tendency to die unexpectedly, and is able to pollute quite a large body of water when decomposing. The swan mussel is the species usually offered. By the way, water snails should not be put in tanks with fish eggs before these have hatched, for the snails will eat the eggs, though not the young fish after hatching.

Pool Problems, Fish Ailments and Remedies

I have mentioned in other places the measures to be taken to ensure that the garden pond does not become a source of trouble and dismay. Prevention of the entry of leaves in autumn and removal of dying foliage on water-lilies and other water plants are elementary precautions to take to avoid fouling of the water. Accumulations of dead leaves in a pool cause an increase in the demands for oxygen at a time when oxygenating plants are dormant, and create conditions harmful to fish and plant life.

Another frequent cause of an unhealthy pool is the rotting of unwanted food given to fish—in a balanced pool with the correct numbers of fish, there should be enough natural food present to keep them in good health. Another cause of cloudy water may be the incorrect use of plant foods, such as an excess of bonemeal or other plant foods in the surface areas of planting areas, instead of putting it in the bottom layers of soil. The appearance of algae, in the form of tangled green filaments which grow rapidly until less robust plants are choked, is usually the result of an excess of nitrogenous matter in the pool, and also of excessive light.

The growth of water-lily leaves and floating aquatics will help to cut down the light, and the introduction of sufficient fish, water snails and the like will help to keep down the increase of algae. Eventually the pool should come to a natural balance and clear itself. Before introducing the fish, the excess algae should be removed. This may be achieved by twisting a stick, through which a few nails have been driven so that they project through the wood, amongst the algae. It will be found that the strands can be wound around the stick drawing them from around the plants until a mass of algae has been collected on the nails. This should be removed from the pool and disposed of on a compost heap. An increase in the number of submerged aquatic plants will also help to keep down algae by competing for the food available. It is not advisable to keep emptying and refilling a pool with fresh water, as this practice encourages the growth of algae, and delays the establishment of a balanced pool, as well as checking the growth of water plants through the low temperature of the new water.

The appearance of cloudiness just after planting a new pool, and sometimes in an established pool in early spring, is usually due to changes in the mineral content of the pool, resulting in very active growth of bacteria and other microscopic organisms. Generally the condition rights itself in two or three weeks' time, when all the various plants begin to grow steadily. If, in spite of patient waiting, the desired results do not come about, there may be the temptation to try chemical means of combating the algae. The old method of using copper sulphate is very effective when used correctly, but there is no room for error, and the slightest overdose will result in the death of all livestock and most of the plants. The recommended dose is 23 grains copper sulphate per 1,000 gallons of water. The crystals are placed in a muslin bag, tied to a long cane and the bag drawn backwards and forwards steadily and slowly, covering the entire area of the pool until the crystals are dissolved. The copper sulphate remains in solution in the water unchanged.

A safer method is to use potassium permanganate, at the rate of ½oz. per 1,000 gallons of water, applied in the same way as the copper sulphate. Applied immediately after planting, it may be repeated later, if necessary, without danger. After application, the water will be purple for a day or two, but the colour will disappear. Again, it is important to use the exact quantity specified. If used too strong, fish will suffer and may be killed, and if too weak, the algae will survive.

These operations should be used as a last resort, only when other methods have not been found successful. The addition of chemicals is bound to affect the balance in the pool. Recently, powerful algicides have become available. These are usually recommended for use in spring before much algal growth appears, and any dead algae must be removed after using it. Any substance which kills algae, which is a green plant, will affect other plants adversely also, if not used strictly according to instructions—clearing a swimming pool is one thing, clearing a lily pool very much another. Incidentally, I had a pool in conditions identical to two more, one on either side of it, the latter being quite clear. This particular pool produced masses of algae for three years in succession in spite of treatment with permanganate. In desperation I bought a bottle of algicide, but before I could use it, the pool suddenly cleared—a case of ESP?

WEEDS

The problem of weed control in small artificial pools, whether by excess growth of oxygenators or by the appearance of rampageous native aquatics (the seeds of which can be introduced by birds and other agencies), is best solved by hand weeding. Generally, it is little trouble to pull out handfuls of oxygenators, sufficient to control the situation, but where permanent strong-rooted weeds have appeared, they should be carefully separated from valued plants and every bit of root extracted. So far as I know there has been developed no herbicide which is sufficiently selective to eliminate unwanted aquatic vegetation without seriously damaging or killing outright valuable plants.

In the case of larger pools, or natural lakes which have got into such a weedy state that a clean sweep is necessary, mechanical weeding by such devices as underwater scythes is but a temporary measure, and the use of herbicides in such cases will be necessary and will give good control. Such pests as duckweed, mare's-tail, water crowfoot, water horsetail, stonewort and blanketweed can be eliminated by suitable treatment with diquat, though often a second treatment may be necessary, as regeneration sometimes occurs. Waterside and marshy areas infested with reeds, giant reed mace (erroneously named bullrush), and invasive grasses respond to treatment with dalapon, though here again often the top growth only is killed, and the rhizomes survive and will require a second or even third treatment to eliminate them completely. After treatment, dead weed must be removed to avoid de-oxygenation of the water, and consequent damage to fish. Diquat and dalapon used in recommended concentrations, according to maker's instructions, will not harm fish or established water-lilies, but if used as a spray, great care must be taken to avoid drift on to neighbouring crops.

If the large pools or natural lakes have an outlet into drainage channels leading into streams and rivers, the local river authority or pollution officer should be notified, before any treatment is carried out, in case there are any local regulations governing the use of such herbicides.

Containers which have contained herbicides or which are only part-used, must be kept securely locked up where children cannot gain access. Empty containers are best burnt.

After the lake is satisfactorily cleaned of weed, any planting operations are best delayed until the following spring to make sure that there is no regeneration, and to allow the possible remnants of herbicide to disintegrate into harmless components.

PESTS AND FUNGUS DISEASES

There are a number of insects which will attack water plants; the commonest is the water-lily aphis, a reddish-black species of greenfly which appears in great numbers, causing discolouration and decay of affected leaves. This species spends part of its life cycle on plum trees. These aphides must be checked as soon as they appear, especially in the indoor pool, or they may be difficult to eradicate. Out of doors the best cure is to hose the insects off the leaves into the surrounding water, where fish will clean them up very efficiently. Indoors, warm water from the pool should be used through a syringe, for hosing from the mains is likely to chill the plants. Alternatively, some form of smoke fumigant might be better, provided that this is guaranteed not to harm fish or plants.

The larvae of the caddis fly occasionally damage water-lily roots and growth buds. These larvae build for themselves protective tubes of grains of sand, bits of plant debris and so forth, cemented together. Their natural foes are fish who will see to it that few survive.

The water-lily beetle is sometimes a destructive pest, damaging flowers and leaves. Eggs are laid on water-lily leaves about mid-summer, and the small, slug-like larvae, dark coloured on top and pale underneath, hatch out in a week and then feed on the leaves. The small brown adult beetles hibernate in the hollow stems of waterside plants, so as a precaution it is wise to cut these down in autumn and burn them. Forcible spraying with a hose will enable fish to clean up the larvae in summer.

The larvae of the brown china marks moth can cause havoc amongst the leaves of water-lilies and other water plants. The eggs are laid near the leaf edges, and the creamy white larvae hatch to feed avidly on the foliage until it goes rotten. Submerging the leaves by flooding will enable fish to eat the eggs or grubs.

Less common is attack by the leaf miner midge, whose larvae disfigure foliage by eating channels through the leaf epidermis. Handpicking as soon as the nuisance is seen is effective. It will be noted that a good fish population in pools is the best safeguard against insect damage.

I mentioned in the last chapter the damage which can be caused by the freshwater whelk, *Limnaea stagnalis*, and a means of reducing the limnaea population. I remember planting two or three dozen *Aponogeton distachyon* in a tank where these beasts were established. They were fine leafy plants, but by the next day there was not a single leaf to be seen. A tender-hearted lady once came to me with a problem. Someone had given her a few limnaeas a few years earlier, and she told me that now she had rows of buckets up and down the garden paths each with a thriving colony of limnaea. She asked me what she could do with them as they were becoming embarrassing.

Ducks and geese are quite incompatible with water gardening, and fine mesh nylon netting, through which their necks cannot penetrate, may protect the plants, but it is better to eat the ducks and geese, and refuse to allow them in the garden again. Once I had a small tank full of *Nymphaea* 'Maurice Laydeker', and at the time my wife kept geese. I covered the tank with chicken netting, but those geese managed to get their heads through and removed every vestige of that rather rare and expensive water-lily.

Occasionally water-lilies are attacked by a fungus which produces a leaf spot. The leaves dry and crumble, spreading the disease until all foliage is killed. Immediate picking and burning of infected leaves may stop the spread of the disease. Spraying with half-strength Bordeaux Mixture, using a fine spray nozzle, and repeating every other day until the disease is controlled, is the recommended treatment, but care must be taken to confine the spray to the foliage, for Bordeaux is a copper fungicide, and too much copper in the water can be harmful. In fact, as a general rule, when spraying insecticides around the garden, or any other sprays, weedkillers and the like, take the greatest care that spray does not drift over the pool. Very small doses of some insecticides, especially those containing derris, are fatal to fish. In addition, any chemical dressings, lawnsands and other possible pollutants, should be kept well away from water gardens, in case they contaminate the water by leaching from surrounding soil. A recent case springs to mind in which household detergent drained into a land-drain which led into a water-lily pool. The result: death of the water-lilies which, of course, happened to be particularly rare kinds.

THE LEAKING POOL

The appearance of cracks in a concrete constructed pool may be attributable to several causes. Failure to ensure a firm, hard foundation before applying the concrete, with consequent uneven settling, and uneven strains building up over the months, is a common cause. Insufficient and variable thickness of concrete walls may result in fracture through ice pressure. Unevenly mixed concrete, use of substandard materials, stale cement, failure to reinforce concrete when this is most advisable, all these may contribute to the appearance of cracks. The use of lime mortar in stone or brick walls of pools, although finished off with cement mortar and rendering, frequently leads to trouble. Any hair cracks in the facing which allow a seepage of water eventually, will cause the lime to be leached away, leaving air gaps under the facing. Frost gets into the cracks and widens them, more water drains away, leaching more mortar, which itself perishes through frost action on the wet mortar, until the only remedy is to knock off all the cement rendering, scrape out all the joints in the walling, and repoint with strong cement-mortar and then reface with strong cement rendering. Cracked pool bottoms caused by uneven settling should be repaired by first breaking up the pool bottom, then ramming the fragments hard, levelling up with broken stone and finally resurfacing with fresh concrete. Hair cracks in concrete walls may be stopped for a while by rubbing in thick, good-quality clay, but eventually they must be made good. Often it is possible to cure them by painting the cracks with one of the specially compounded plastic paints. If the cracks are too wide for this treatment, they may be cleaned out thoroughly and filled up with fibre-glass and then painted over with plastic paint. Fibre-glass repairs usually last well. Cement-filled crevices often crack again within a short time, for it is impossible to bond new and old cement work satisfactorily. In such a case, the only way is to widen the cracks with a chisel, chip over the entire old surface of the pool with a small pick or chisel, fill up the cracks with a strong sand-cement mix, and then re-render the entire pool with a $\frac{1}{2}$-in. thickness of strong, fine concrete with a waterproofing compound added. After these repairs, it will be necessary to re-season the pool before introducing plants or fish. When the leak is caused by the swelling of tree roots below the pool, fracturing the pool bottom, and also probably lifting the sides, it is not of permanent benefit to try and patch the concrete, for the cause will remain active so long as the roots live. Either write off the pool to experience or, if there is no other site, line the pool with a plastic liner or with plastic-treated hessian surfaced with the correct plastic paint. Such a lining will give way to the swelling roots without rupture and last several years.

The above remarks may seem to suggest that concrete pools are always a source of trouble, but this is not so, if they are constructed correctly and sited away from trees. I know of concrete pools, which were made 30 years ago, and which still give no trouble at all. Tears in plastic pools may be repaired by applying patches to the cleaned surfaces, with the appropriate plastic liner material and the adhesive recommended for that particular liner. Or, if it is beginning to perish, replace the liner with a new one. During these operations, provision should be made to accommodate plants and fish in suitable containers until the pool is ready for their return.

FISH AILMENTS AND ENEMIES

Like any other living organism, fish are by no means immune to attack by various diseases and parasites, to say nothing of their fellow creatures. It is well said that prevention is better than cure and, in the first place, it is essential to provide the correct environment. Supposing that there is a well-established water garden in being, with healthy plants growing satisfactorily, perhaps the first matter to consider is how many fish should be admitted to the pool. I have mentioned this earlier but it will bear repetition. The amount of oxygen available in a pool is directly proportional to the water surface, the oxygen supplied by submerged oxygenating plants is available only during sunshine, not at night, during dull weather or when the plants are dormant in winter. The maximum quantity of fish which can be supported has been established at 1in. of fish, excluding fins, per 3sq. in. of water surface for cold water fish—in heated tanks allow 6sq. in. surface per 1in. of fish. The depth of the pool has little or no effect on the oxygen exchange, except, of course, that the deeper pool has a greater storage capacity for oxygen than the shallower one. When fish spend a lot of time at the surface blowing bubbles, they are not trying to communicate with their owner, but almost certainly are short of oxygen, and the pool is either overstocked or there is some other trouble.

When fish are being introduced into the pool, the water in their container should be brought up—or down—to the pool temperature, by immersing the container in the pool until the temperatures in the container and pool are equal. Sudden changes of temperature cause severe shock to fish and actually cause damage such as congested fins. Newly acquired fish may already have the seeds of disease, and it is a wise precaution to treat them accordingly. In any case they will have suffered some shock through transit from the source of supply. A bath of weak potassium permanganate at the strength of $\frac{1}{4}$ grain to 1gal. water for about two hours should clear the fish of any disease germs or spores, and render them innocuous to the established denizens of the pool. Any nets or other equipment should receive the same treatment.

Signs of trouble in fish are drooping fins, sluggishness, congested fins, and slimy excrement containing bubbles. Fish showing these symptoms should be isolated and treated as soon as possible, remembering always that sudden temperature changes are dangerous. Ailing fish should not be given any food at all, and they should be kept in a shady place. One of the best treatments for poorly fish is to place them in salt water. Clean seawater (1 part) mixed with 5 parts of fresh water is recommended, the mixture being changed daily. Failing seawater, 2 teaspoonfuls of pure salt to 1gal. water will serve. Two or three days of this treatment usually brings back to health most off-colour fish. The potassium permanganate treatment for newly acquired fish also is very good; after two days remove the fish to plain water, and repeat after 10 days' interval if thought necessary.

Specific troubles which affect fish are constipation, fin congestion, gill congestion, tail congestion, tail rot, tuberculosis, injuries to eyes and scales, fungus diseases, white spot, and attacks from the larvae of dragon-flies, the giant diving beetle and other aquatic larvae, anchor worm and fish flukes. This is quite an impressive list, but one may keep fish for years without meeting more than one or two of these troubles.

CONSTIPATION

Symptoms are sluggishness and unhealthy excrement, slimy and containing bubbles (healthy excrement is usually seen as brown more or less lengthy pieces). Caused often by overfeeding with artificial foods. Transfer to a container with a solution of ½oz salt and ½oz Epsom Salts to 1gal. of water, for two days. Or drop two or three drops of castor oil down the gullet of the fish and return it to the pool.

GILL CONGESTION

The gills swell and inflame, and become discoloured with a grey-white film. Usually fatal, and may be infectious. A two-day immersion in the salt bath may or may not cure. Three to four drops of Dettol in 1gal. of water is a good disinfectant. The fish should not be left in this solution more than 10 minutes, but a second treatment a day later may be tried.

TAIL AND FIN CONGESTION

The fins become bloodshot, and may split. If the condition spreads to the body it usually is fatal. May be caused by overcrowding, overfeeding or temperature shocks. The salt water treatment is good but, if not effective, try penicillin, at 15,000 units per gallon. This treatment usually cures the trouble, and is harmless to fish. Provide better conditions and feed more sparingly, preferably with live foods.

TAIL ROT

The tail fin begins to split and becomes ragged. If the condition reaches the body it is likely to be fatal. Try the salt water treatment. The ragged portions may be cut away by holding the fish in a soft damp cloth against a wet smooth surface and trimming with a sharp knife, afterwards dabbing the cut edges with 0·5 per cent permanganate solution. Or try the penicillin treatment, also at 15,000 units per gallon of water. If not effective a stronger solution may cure the trouble.

TUBERCULOSIS

The fish wastes away, stops eating and swimming, and is best destroyed, as the condition is very difficult to arrest or cure.

FUNGUS DISEASE

Water usually contains spores of a dangerous fungus disease, *Saprolegnia ferox*, but this seldom infects healthy or undamaged fish. The fungus appears as a white film, first on the fins, and then spreading over the body. When the gills are affected, the fish usually dies. The old salt treatment is effective, starting with two teaspoons salt to 1gal. of water, gradually increasing the salt to ½oz. to 1gal. over a period of two days. The salt additions should be dissolved in water first and well stirred into the bath. A quicker method is to prepare a solution of malachite green, at the rate of 4 grains per gallon, in a clean container. Transfer the fish to this solution for not more than half a minute and then return the fish to the pool. In very bad cases where several fish are affected, remove all the fish for treatment in a clean separate container, and disinfect the pool with a strong permanganate solution. Submerged aquatics may be killed by the strong solution, and should be replaced with new, clean plants. It is wise to disinfect new plants with weak permanganate solution before planting in the pool.

WHITE SPOT

This appears as a rash of small white spots covering the body of the affected fish. These spots are tiny parasites, which imbed themselves in the fish and, when mature, drop to the bottom of the pool, whence they proceed to infect more fish. It usually attacks tropical fish only but may affect others in warm water tanks, and can infect cold water fish. First symptoms are the fish rubbing themselves against plants and other objects and then the white spots appear. As white spot is very infectious, any affected fish should be removed at once to another tank for treatment. Add five drops of 2½ per cent mercurochrome to 1gal. of water in the treatment tank, introduce the affected fish, and gradually heat up the water to 80 °F. (27 °C.); keep it at this temperature for a week, after which the parasites should be killed. Allow the tank to cool down gradually to the temperature of the pool and return the fish to it. If badly infected, the whole pool may have to be treated, and in this case it is better to use quinine hydrochloride at the rate of 2 grains to 1gal. of water, dissolving the quinine in water first and adding to the pool in three or four doses spread over a day. This concentration will not harm the plants, and the water need not be changed afterwards as the quinine will gradually break down. Each addition of quinine solution should be stirred well into the pool so as to avoid local concentrations.

INJURIES TO EYES AND SCALES

The eyes of goldfish, particularly those of the fancy varieties, telescopes and celestials, may be injured on their way from the suppliers, or from knocks received when swimming amongst obstacles in the pool. In mild cases, a simple swabbing with standard boric acid solution should clear up the trouble, but in bad cases drops of an iodine preparation may be more effective. This is made up of 2 parts standard iodine solution in 98 parts glycerine. The dose is two drops directed into the damaged eye. The fish should be held in a wet soft cloth, not in the uncovered hand, which would cause discomfort to the fish. Nets should be of fine mesh material, coarse nets may injure the fish. In the case of damaged scales and abrasions, swab the affected part with the iodine glycerine mixture, followed by a bath in the saltwater tank. The saltwater treatment may be sufficient in itself.

FISH LICE

Small crustaceans, about the size of pinheads, which attach themselves to the fish body and gills, causing acute distress. They may be removed by touching each one with one drop of kerosene (paraffin), applied with a small camelhair brush. As a rule they will drop off at a touch. Usually they are introduced with wild plants. A badly infested pool should be treated with permanganate, ¼ grain to the gallon, dissolved beforehand in some suitable vessel and well distributed through the pool. This concentration will not harm the fish for a day or so. Half the water may then be siphoned away and replaced with clean water.

FLUKES

Minute parasites attaching themselves to the gills causing great distress, exhaustion, emaciation and death. They may be seen with a hand lens as tiny threadlike bodies. Affected fish should be removed and treated in an isolation tank containing 20 drops commercial formaldehyde to the gallon, but they must be removed after 10 minutes. Repeat the dose three days in succession. Alternatively, use a bath containing 5 drops Dettol to 1gal. of water, remove fish after 10 minutes—no longer—and repeat the following day. If many fish are affected treat the pool with permanganate as for fish lice.

A dropping bottle should be used to measure out the required dose as it is too easy to exceed the safe dose otherwise.

SWIMMING BLADDER TROUBLE

Usually affects fancy goldfish, which have been overfed and become subject to digestive upsets. The fish cannot swim in the correct position and become erratic in their movements. Difficult to cure, but there are proprietary remedies to be had which may help.

INSECT ENEMIES

Every pool is subject to invasion by various insect pests, especially those whose larvae spend their larval state under water. One of the chief enemies is the great diving beetle, which flies at night, migrating from pool to pool, diving into any sheet of water it comes across. Frequently the beetle is misled by the gleam of moonlight on glasshouses and I have often been startled when slug hunting at night by a loud rap as one of these beasts tries to dive through the glass. The adult beetle will attack fish fiercely. Watch the pool and net every beetle you see and destroy it. They are quite easy to see, as they come up to the surface to renew their air supply at frequent intervals. They are about 1¾in. long, dark blackish brown in colour with a narrow yellow border. Their eggs are laid within the tissues of water plants, and the larvae— the water tigers—are vicious attackers of fish also. Dragonflies are harmless and beautiful as they hover over the pool, but their larvae are aquatic, predacious and will attack and suck out the juices of fish. They have a kind of hinged, pincer-tipped mandible, which they shoot out and fasten on to an unsuspecting fish. Two inches long, olive brown and hard to spot, they are jet propelled. Handpicking is the only practicable method of getting rid of them. There are other predacious beetle larvae, such as that of the water scavenger beetle, roundish 3-in. menaces which lie in wait for unwary fish. A bottle with a neck too narrow for fish to enter, and bated with a little raw meat, submerged on the pool bottom may catch a few, but handpicking is the best way of controlling them.

Larger enemies include rats, cats, herons, kingfishers—if you are lucky enough to have these beautiful birds in your neighbourhood—and the young of *Homo sapiens*. The pool can be netted if the birds begin to visit your pool; once they find it they will call again and again until they have accounted for all the fish. Near the coast seabirds also can clean up a fish pond very well. Rats should be trapped or eradicated by poison. Youngsters invariably take a keen interest in a garden pool, but by patience and understanding plus information on the habits and needs of the inhabitants, it should be possible to deter too enthusiastic investigation of the pool, and perhaps recruit a new generation of pondowners, with a lifelong interest for their leisure hours.

Where very young children might fall into lily pools, possibly with tragic results, the only real safeguard is to net over the pool. Green, plastic-covered sheep netting is not too conspicuous. It should be secured to firm stakes. In the case of a formally shaped pool, a built-in underwater net could be installed 2 or 3in. below the surface. This would not be seen, and the plants would grow through the meshes. Ring-bolts or hooks cemented into the side walls just below the water surface would enable the netting to be kept taut. In the case of plastic pools, however, the overall net would be the only practical one to install.

When winter comes, make sure that there are no leaves lying in the pond to rot and start trouble. Protect pumps from frost damage either by draining the pumping system or by supplying adequate insulation to the pump chamber without preventing air circulation. Check electric installations and make good any doubtful sections. If the pool is too shallow to ensure ample water below the frost level, where fish can winter unharmed, consider installing an immersion heater designed to keep a small area unfrozen. Ponds 2 or more feet deep are unlikely to freeze solid in England. If dangerously shallow, it might be wise to winter the fish in adequate indoor tanks. Any tender aquatics planted outside for the summer should be lifted, and placed in appropriate frost-free quarters not later than October. There seems little else to worry about, and one can relax and look forward to the next season of interest and charm from the water garden.

M

Some Suppliers

British Isles

'Bennetts' Water Lily & Fish Farm, Chickerell, Weymouth, Dorset.
Highland Water Gardens, Rickmansworth, Herts.
Newlake Gardens, Copthorne, Crawley, Sussex.
G. B. Perry's Hardy Plant Farm, Enfield, Middlesex.
Stewart's Nurseries Ltd., Ringwood, Hants.
Waitham Nurseries, Silverdale, Carnforth, Lancs.

U.S.A.

Glendale Flower and Water Gardens, 1260 Justin Ave., Glendale, Calif.
Nolt's Ponds, Silver Spring, Pa.
Slocum Water Gardens, 950 Front St., Binghamton, N.Y.
Three Springs Fisheries, 838 Main Road, Lilypons, Maryland.
Van Ness Water Gardens, Route 1, Box 339, Upland, Calif.
William Tricker, Inc., 7228 Rainbow Terrace, Independence, Oregon, and Saddle River, N.J.

France

Latour-Marliac, Temple-sur-Lot, France.

Index

King Cup, see *Caltha*
Kirengshoma
Knotweed, see *Polygonum*
Koi, 160

Lady Fern, see *Athyrium*
Lagarosiphon, see *Elodea*
Leaf miner midge, 169
Leaf spot, 169
Leaks, dealing with, 170–1
Lemna, 72, 122
Lemon Apple, see *Podophyllum*
Leucojum, 140
Ligularia, 140–1
Limnaea, 107, 163, 169
Limnanthemum, 69, 112
Limnobium, 128
Limnocharis, see *Hydrocleys*
Lionhead, 162
Lizard's Tail, see *Saururus*
Lobelia, 112–13
Loosestrife, see *Lythrum*
Lotus, 91, 104
Ludwigia, 113
Lysichitum, 69, 113
Lythrum, 141–2

Male Fern, see *Dryopteris*
Manna Grass, see *Glycerium*
Marestail, see *Hippuris*
Mariscus, see *Cyperus*
Marsh Cinquefoil, see *Potentilla*
Marsh Marigold, see *Caltha*
Marsh St. John's Wort, see *Hypericum*
Marsh Trefoil, see *Menyanthes*
Matteuccia, 132
May Apple, see *Podophyllum*
Menyanthes, 113–14
Micranthes see *Saxifraga*
Michaelmas Daisy, see *Aster*
Mimulus, 142–3
Miscanthus, 154
Monarda, 143
Monkey Flower, see *Mimulus*
Moor, telescopic, 162
Mountain Buckler Fern, see *Oreopteris*
Mouse Ear, see *Myosotis*
Myriophyllum, 126, 130

Myosotis, 114

Nelumbo, 101–2
Nesaea, see *Decodon*
Ness gardens, 133
Nuphar, 102–4
Nymph, 163
Nymphaea. Hardy species and cultivars, 78–88
  marliacea 'Chromatella', 34
  Tender species and cultivars, 89–99
    Day-blooming cultivars, 93–6
    night-blooming, 96–8
  Tropical species, 90–3
  tuberosa 'Poestlingberg', 33, 88
Nymphoides, see *Limnanthemum*

Oenanthe, 126
Onoclea, 133
Oranda, 162
Oreopteris, 133
Orfe, golden and silver, 159
Orontium, 69, 114
Osmunda, 133
Ostrich Feather Fern, see *Matteuccia*
Oswego Tea, see *Monarda*
Oxygenators for outdoor pools, 124–7
  for tropical pools, 127–30

Pampas Grass, see *Cortaderia*
Papyrus, see *Cyperus*
Parrots-feather Milfoil, see *Myriophyllum*
Peltandra, 114–15
Peltiphyllum, 143–4
Penthorum, 115
Petasites, 143
Phalaris, 154–5
Pickerel Weed, see *Pontederia*
Pigmy Weed, see *Tillaea*
Phyllanthus, 128
Pistia, 123
Podophyllum, 144
Polapool, 27–8
Polygonum, 144
Polythene, 24–5
Pond Lily, see *Nuphar*
Pond snails, 163